ISBN 978-1-5284-4062-2
PIBN 10924247

This book is a reproduction of an important historical work. Forgotten Books uses state-of-the-art technology to digitally reconstruct the work, preserving the original format whilst repairing imperfections present in the aged copy. In rare cases, an imperfection in the original, such as a blemish or missing page, may be replicated in our edition. We do, however, repair the vast majority of imperfections successfully; any imperfections that remain are intentionally left to preserve the state of such historical works.

English
Français
Deutsche
Italiano
Español
Português

www.forgottenbooks.com

Mythology Photography **Fiction**
Fishing Christianity **Art** Cooking
Essays Buddhism Freemasonry
Medicine **Biology** Music **Ancient
Egypt** Evolution Carpentry Physics
Dance Geology **Mathematics** Fitness
Shakespeare **Folklore** Yoga Marketing
Confidence Immortality Biographies
Poetry **Psychology** Witchcraft
Electronics Chemistry History **Law**
Accounting **Philosophy** Anthropology
Alchemy Drama Quantum Mechanics
Atheism Sexual Health **Ancient History**
Entrepreneurship Languages Sport
Paleontology Needlework Islam
Metaphysics Investment Archaeology
Parenting Statistics Criminology
Motivational

JANUARY 1925.

UNITED STATES DEPARTMENT OF AGRICULTURE
FOREST SERVICE
WASHINGTON D.C.

T H E   F O R E S T   W O R K E R

January, 1925

Published bimonthly by the Forest Service, U. S. Department
of Agriculture, Washington, D. C.

C O N T E N T S

Meeting of American Forestry Association

The annual meeting of the American Forestry Association, which will also be its semi-centennial, will be held on January 22, 1925, at the Hamilton Club, Chicago, Illinois, with the Illinois Forestry Association as host.

The American Forestry Association was organized in Chicago in 1875, and for that reason the 1925 meeting will be held there. Mr. William L. Hall of Chicago, a member of both associations, is Chairman of the Committee on General Arrangements, and has arranged a program featuring:

 (1) Forest interests of Illinois.

 (2) How maximum cooperation in forest fire protection may be developed under the Clarke-McNary Law.

 (3) An enlarged program of forest land purchases under the Weeks Law as enlarged by the Clarke-McNary Law.

- - - - - - -

A Correction

On page 6 of the November issue of "The Forest Worker" there appeared an erroneous statement regarding the "Forestry Contract Act for Georgia," in which it was stated that the act recently became a law in Georgia, whereas the bill was killed in the Assembly.

Annual Meeting of the Southern Forestry Congress

You are invited to attend the Seventh Forestry Congress to be held in Little Rock, Arkansas, January 19-21, 1925, at the Marion Hotel.

A very interesting program is being arranged including:

State Forestry Legislation.
Forestry Problems in Shortleaf Pine.
Forestry Problems in Hardwood.
Louisiana and Arkansas Hardwoods.
Paper and Pulpwood in the South.
Forestry and Naval Stores.

SOUTHERN FORESTRY CONGRESS

C. B. Harman, Secretary.

. . . .

. . . .

"As Others See Us"

Con

"The Forest Worker" received. Its attempts at humor are strictly mid-western, if not mid-Victorian. Can't you help put more pep and orderliness in it? It seems a jumble of unrelated paragraphs. It doesn't seem to be impressing itself much in this District."
(Extract from a letter from one Forest Service man to another.)

Pro

"The Forest Worker" has just some and has made a very good impression in every way. It is particularly interesting perhaps as heralding the fast-coming change in Government publications from something dry-as-dust to a humanized document with a nicely developed vein of humor running through it. Greatstuff!"--(Extract from a letter from a Canadian forester.)

Our skin is thick and our vanity easily tickled, hence criticisms and comments of all kinds are gladly received. We especially welcome helpful constructive criticisms.

. . . .

STATE FOREST DEPARTMENTS AND ORGANIZATIONS

Speaks on Conservation in Arkansas

In an address on "The Conservation of Forest Resources in Arkansas" delivered at the Arkansas State Fair, Dr. A. C. Millar, who is secretary of the honorary forestry commission of Arkansas, appointed by Gov. T. J. McRae to study the forest situation in Arkansas, called attention to the absolute necessity of conserving our national timber resources which the American people have assumed were inexhaustible.

After explaining the occasion for Gov. McRae's appointment of the honorary forestry commission, Dr. Millar specified four principal problems requiring solution, as follows: (1) the protection of our forests from destructive fires; (2) a system of equitable taxation that will protect the owners against prohibitive taxes on the growing timber, while it yields a fair tax from the land itself and a deferred tax from the timber when cut; (3) provision for creating State and National Forests, and (4) a plan to encourage the small owner to maintain a perpetual woodlot.

To prevent fires there must be provision for organizing and educating the people so that every citizen may become intelligently interested and ready for cooperative service. As a solution of the second problem he suggested that the State should enter into a contract to tax only the land values during the process of growth, and then collect an equitable tax from the timber when it is mature or is cut. He further advocated that lands valueless for other purposes should be purchased at nominal prices and converted into National and State forests. Woodlots, it was pointed out, may become a source of perpetual profit to both the farmer and the State, since the income to be gained from one lot may exceed that from almost any other kind of farming.

Dr. Millar closed his address with an appeal for intelligent and hearty cooperation on the part of the citizens of the State when the Arkansas honorary forestry commission presents its recommendations to the State legislature for adoption. --American Lumberman.

(Due to the work of the Honorary Forestry Commission of Arkansas last summer, the January session of the Arkansas State Legislature will doubtless have before it a bill embodying the creation of a State Forestry Department and an organized fire protection system which will enable the State to qualify for the cooperative funds distributed under the Weeks Law and the Clarke-McNary Law.)--Ed.

One Won and One Lost in Minnesota

The referendum vote upon the proposed amendment to the Constitution of the State of Minnesota, known as Amendment #4, authorizing the enactment of laws for the encouragement and promotion of forestation of lands in the State, whether owned by private persons or the public, including "irrepealable provisions for definite and limited taxation of such lands during a term of years, and for a yield tax at or after the end of such term, upon the timber and other forest products so grown," was submitted to the people of Minnesota upon November 4, 1924, and defeated. This was not due to the votes against it, but rather to the lack of interest of people voting.

Amendment #5, permitting the State and its political subdivisions, when authorized by the Legislature to contract debts and pledge the public credit for and engage in any work reasonably tending to prevent or abate forest fires, including the compulsory clearing and improvement of wild lands (whether publicly or privately owned), and also providing for the assessment against such land of the value of all benefits so conferred and the payment of damages so sustained in excess of such benefits, voted upon at the same time as Amendment #4, was carried.--G. M. Conzet, State Forester.

- - - - - - -

New York State Park Bond Issue Wins

The election on November 4 resulted in a substantial victory for the $15,000,000 bond issue to be used for the continued support of existing State parks and for extensive purchase of new park areas.

One-third of the proposed bond issue, $5,000,000, goes to the extension of the Adirondack and Catskill forest preserves by the Conservation Commission. Maintenance of forest cover in these regions, it is said, is vitally necessary to protect their streams from drying up and from pollution. Eventually these preserves may become sources of timber for commercial use, but for the present their principal value is for water, hunting, fishing, camping, tramping, and mountain climbing - a three-million-acre playground for the people of the densely populated areas of the State. -- American Forests and Forest Life.

- - - - - - -

Amendment Carried in Wisconsin

The referendum vote upon the proposed amendment of section 10 of article 8 of the Constitution of Wisconsin, authorizing the State to appropriate moneys for the acquirement of land for State forest purposes, was submitted to the people of Wisconsin upon November 4, 1924, and carried, with approximately 65 per cent of the voters having expressed themselves on this item.--C. L. Harrington, Supt. of State Forests and Parks, Madison, Wis.

Washington Considers Forest Taxation

The keynote of discussion at the Fourth Washington State Forestry Conference held in Seattle, Washington on November 21, under the auspices of the Forestry Committee of the Seattle Chamber of Commerce, was "How Should Forest Lands be Taxed?"

The forest land taxation committee, which has been studying the question of timber taxation now for several years, made an interesting report with definite recommendations for State forest tax legislation to be introduced in the January session of the State legislature. In brief, the bill to be presented provides:

1. All forest land shall be assessed at a valuation based on the value of the land for the production of timber. In making the assessment the State supervisor of taxation, as advised by the State forest board, shall furnish each county assessor with a schedule of values of land to conform with the above and the county assessor shall be guided by this schedule of values and limited by the maximum and minimum rates so fixed. Any improvements or value other than forest value shall be assessed in addition to the value of the land in accordance with existing laws.

2. All forest crops shall be taxed uniformly at the tax rate prevailing in the district of assessment under the following conditions:

When immature forests, or those under 70 years of age, as determined by the State forester, are cut in whole or in part, a yield tax shall be applied in the following manner: The owner or owners shall report to the assessor each quarter in thousands of board feet the amount of material removed and this will be entered on the rolls and assessed at the same rate as matured standing timber, this tax being the only tax assessed. Timber 70 years or more of age which has been and is being regularly assessed as standing timber for taxation purposes shall not be additionally assessed on any other basis, but the land will continue to be valued as in Section 1.

3. Owners of land suitable for forest production desiring to grow forest crops may enter into a contract with the State for a definite period of years whereby they place their lands in the reforestation class to be managed under reforestation plans and policies approved by the State supervisor of forests, and subjecting themselves thereby to the terms and conditions of the laws of the State with reference to fire protection and reforestation. In all contracts so entered into valuations as stated in Section 2 of the act and the valuations as determined in accordance with Section 1 shall become a part of the contract.

Taxation and reforestation of logged-off lands is now recognized as one of the most important problems of the State of Washington. A bill creating a definite forest policy for the State was adopted at the last session of the legislature as a result of the activities of the State Forestry Conference.

Dean Hugo Winkenwerder, of the College of Forestry, University of Washington, was chairman of the conference and arranged the program. Among the resolutions adopted were these:

Urging the State legislature to appropriate at least $30,000 annually for forest research work under the direction of the University of Washington college of forestry; endorsing the fire warning weather forecasts of the United States Weather Bureau and urging their continuance and extension; urging the passage of adequate appropriations under the Clarke-McNary Law; urging army airplane forest fire patrols in this section, and pledging the State legislature the full support of the conference in all constructive forestry legislation.--Condensed from various sources.

- - - - - -

Recreational Use of Forests

Participation in recreational use is not only a forester's privilege, it is his duty. We are in the pioneer stage of forestry in America. The profession will necessarily continue pioneering until sound forest practice is exemplified generally throughout the United States. One of the most gratifying developments in our work has been the increasing recognition by the public of the urgency and wisdom of forest production and utilization on a scientific basis. The temper of the public is to have forest devastation stopped and to utilize as fully as practicable all products of the forest. This attitude of the public mind is attributable to many factors, not the least important of which is the regard held by the American for trees and forest values for those intangible benefits which mean to him better health, better recreation and a more attractive environment. No element of our people has worked more persistently for better tree and forest appreciation than those whose dominant goal is the broad public interest rather than commitment to a higher forest technique. The forester has been most fortunate in having the confidence of this and other classes, earnest in their appeal for better forests, in his attempt to have sound forest practice adopted. Whether he will or no, the forester is definitely identified in this country with outdoor recreation. He should be thoroughly grateful for this wide opportunity for public service. --R. Y. Stuart, Sec'y Penn. Dept. of Forests and Waters in Penn. Service Letter.

- - - - - - - - -

A Color Problem

(How to Get White Paper from Yellow Pine by the Brown Paper Company)

A few months ago the Monroe News Star printed a rather unusual edition in the interests of industrial activity of North Louisiana. The newspaper was printed on Kraft paper made in Monroe, Louisiana, by the Brown Paper Company. Forty-eight hours before the edition was published the paper on which it was printed was in the form of small logs, branches, and trunks of small trees, and was piled in large stacks in the receiving yard of the paper company.

The possibilities of the paper-making industry in Louisiana loom larger and larger as research in this product develops. In times past there have been isolated instances where a flat-bed press has used Kraft paper for a special edition. This is the first instance in which a high-speed rotary press has used Kraft paper for any edition. Chemists at present have not been able to solve a cheap commercial process for bleaching this paper white. The paper as manufactured varies from a deep brown to a light brown. It would not serve the newspaper industry for regular editions because it is difficult to read and a strain on the eyes, but foresters and paper makers are very optimistic and believe that ultimately a method will be worked out through chemical research for the bleaching of this paper to a white surface at a reasonable cost. When this comes to pass Louisiana will enjoy a tremendous prosperity through the pulp industry which has been established in the past few years.

The basic material for the manufacture of paper is pine pulp. Trees for pulp wood can be grown in 7 to 15 years on lands not fit for agriculture. Louisiana has 13,500,000 acres of idle cut-over lands which can supply the generations to come with vast supplies of wood for pulp wood. To grow pulp successfully, forest fires must be eliminated. The basic problem of reforestation is the elimination of forest fires which, if adhered to, means the growing of a new crop of timber for pulp, and the development of forest products industry which will contribute greatly to the future industrial prosperity of Louisiana.—Louisiana Conservation News.

- - - - - - -

Formulate New Forestry Legislation

A meeting of State and Federal forestry officials and representatives of the lumber industry of Montana was held at Missoula recently to formulate a more comprehensive code of forestry laws for presentation to the next legislature, aimed to protect present forests and insure as far as may be the perpetuation of the lumber industry in the State.--The Timberman.

- - - - - - -

Trees for Reforestation

A total of 620,150 trees were shipped from our New York State nurseries this fall. Most of these were purchased by individuals, although some were planted by municipalities, fish and game clubs, camps, schools, etc. The total distribution of trees from the nurseries for 1924 will be about 9,115,000 trees. This is a new record for this State in reforesting.

We already have on file for spring delivery a large number of tree orders, aggregating some 825,000 trees. In addition to this we will receive on January 1 orders covering the allotment of 500,000 trees, which are to be granted to the counties of the State for demonstration plantings under the direction of the various farm bureaus.—N.Y. Observer.

- - - - - -

Forestry Practice and Vision

Thirty years cover the total age of American Forestry. In that period only the old-timers can wholly appreciate how high in achievement and promise the profession has climbed. In the old ignorant and scornful days the forester almost foreswore his ideals lest he be called a foolish visionary. Now, not only the unmistakable demands of the future, but the very business needs of to-day require him to be a man of vision. Timber is not the only one of the natural resources by which we live that is nearing a predictable end, but it is one of the few that is replaceable, and its immense influence on our standards of living no longer has to be proved. Where once – and not so long ago – the question was where to buy stumpage, the question now is how to grow it.

From now on we are going to be asked to produce timber crops. We must bring our silviculture out of hiding and put it to work. Let us be sure – for the sake of our jobs – that it will work, but let us be sure also that we know its wider meanings. For the true forester it is not a set of immediate prescriptions and expedients, however practical they may be; it is a minute and growing knowledge of the life of a particular forest, its past, its future, and the ideal of composition and productiveness that is always obscured by the conditions of the present. It means more and more insight into the working of those natural factors that are lasting, like soil and water, and that may be in large part controlled by the forest itself. Finally, it means a long look ahead to all the human uses that the ultimate forest may fulfill. It is the exercise of this kind of vision that in the years soon to come will make the forester all the better a business man, and that makes his profession one of the most rewarding in existence. —R. T. Fisher, Director, Harvard Forest School, Penn. Service Letter.

To Cure the Ill in Illinois

One of the very interesting and instructive exhibits at the Illinois Products Exposition held in Chicago recently was that of the Scientific Surveys, State of Illinois, which was arranged by R. B. Miller, State Forester, and presented in miniature the forestry situation in Illinois. This display was in three parts, one showing the amount of wood needed for various purposes on the average Illinois farm; another showing the actual amount of wood grown on woodlots of the State; and the third showing the amount that with sound forestry methods could be grown.

It was indicated that the chief products of the farm woodlot are posts, ties and cord wood; the figures given being based in part on questionnaires and in part on surveys actually made on the ground. Of the 2,353,662,000 board feet of lumber consumed in the State annually, 2,310,453,000 feet is imported and 43,209,000 is home grown and consumed within the State. Native woods are chiefly hardwoods.--American Lumberman.

- - - - - - -

To the Industrial Workers of Louisiana

Statistics on the cost of producing lumber show that for every $100 spent for lumber, $90.00 goes to the labor necessary to remove same from the stump to the consumer. What action are you taking in protecting the natural resource that gives you 90 per cent of its manufactured value as a means of making a living? Carelessness is the greatest of all factors causing the destructive forest fires. You protect your homes against fires, why not help us protect the product that means a good living to you?

What are you doing to prevent forest fires?--La. Conservation News.

- - - - - - -

Bad Autumn Fire Season in East

The droughty weather that prevailed for many weeks over a considerable part of the country east of the Rocky Mountains, particularly in the New England and North Atlantic States, had the usual effect of increasing the fire hazard in forests. In consequence of a special forecast issued by the Weather Bureau for the Adirondack region, indicating that no rain was in prospect, the Governor of New York State took the unprecedented step of closing, by executive order, both the Adirondacks and the Catskills to campers and hunters until further notice. A statement issued in connection with the Governor's proclamation declared that more than 40 fires had occurred since the preceding week, which "seriously threatened all the forests" in those regions. The order affected only the so-called "fire towns" in each forest preserve, which are a popular resort of hunters and picnickers. --Official Record.

- - - - - - -

Prosperity of Georgia Depends Upon Its Timber Supply

The prosperity of Georgia, as well as every other State in the Union, depends upon what its citizens are able to secure or produce from the ground. For the past fifty years or more our lumber and naval stores have netted us an average of about fifteen million dollars a year.

~~~ e of New York spent more than two million dollars last year on purchase, protection and maintenance of forest land; the State of Pennsylvania, $683,000; Massachusetts, $427,000; Michigan, $324,000; Maine, $210,000; Minnesota, $196,000; Ohio, $159,000; Washington, $163,000; and twenty-three other States sums from $2,000 to $87,000. All told, thirty-two States spent $5,410,119 on forestry. Every State in the South except Georgia, Florida, and South Carolina has concentrated its forces against the forest fire evil and in ten years, unless we do the same at once, we shall be buying 50 per cent, if not more, of our lumber from them.

The essentials necessary now are fire protection, standard taxation on land for a definite period, deferred taxes on growing timber until cut or worked, a State forestry board with a number of assistant foresters sufficient to advise and inform the public, and the necessary money to maintain such an organization.---C. B. Harman, Sec'y, Southern Forestry Association in AGRICULTURAL BULLETIN, Atlanta and West Point R. R. Co., Western Railway of Alabama, Georgia Railroad.

- - - - - - -

Will Study Maryland's Lumber Needs

The Maryland Department of Forestry is planning investigations to determine the quantity of lumber used annually in the State and its ratio to the amount produced there. It will also seek to determine the lumber-producing possibilities of the State in order to ascertain the forestry development necessary to make Maryland self-sustaining in this commodity. In this connection F. W. Besley, State Forester, pointed out that investigations made by the Department show approximately four-fifths of the lumber used in Maryland to be brought in from outside sources at an outlay annually for freight alone of not less than 5 million dollars. This item, Mr. Besley contends, could be lopped off the freight bill if all of the lumber used were turned out from forests within the borders of Maryland. The average freight haul on lumber was found to be about 475 miles.--American Lumberman.

- - - - - - -

North Carolina on Exhibit in New York

The North Carolinian who is in New York in January and who visits the Southern Exposition to be held at the Grand Central Palace will be able to imagine himself "Down Home," from whatever section of the State he may hail.

A travelogue film, which is being made by the Motion Picture Arts, Inc., of Greensboro, North Carolina, in pursuance with a contract recently signed by the North Carolina Geological and Economic Survey, will include views of the three sections, Mountains, Piedmont, and Coastal Plain. In turn these will be represented by pictures of their more striking and illuminating features, both physical and vocational. In form the motion picture will be run in the familiar manner of scenes from a moving automobile, so that whatever is shown as the indicative finger follows the journey on the map of the State, the outstanding exhibit of North Carolina's now nationally famous highways will always be present.

The film, in addition to making a novel and very attractive part of the exhibit, will be the permanent property of the State and of high value as a record.--N.C. Natural Resources.

- - - - - - -

Idaho to Travel on the Clarke-McNary Train

Idaho's forest fire laws are admittedly weak as regards the protection of cut-over lands, and adequate protection here is the key to a future timber supply. Idaho, therefore, in order to share the increased appropriations proposed by the Clarke-McNary Law for cooperative fire protection must so amend her forestry laws as to insure permanency in timber growing on State and private lands. To enable the State to take advantage of the various provisions of the Clarke-McNary Law, the North Idaho Chamber of Commerce and the South Idaho Commercial Clubs have appointed a committee of fourteen members to formulate a forest policy in line with the needs of the entire State.

On the committee are represented the irrigation interests, the stock growers, the lumber industry, the merchants, the State and Federal Government. The committee has for some months been studying the States' needs in the way of forest legislation, has held numerous meetings, and is now formulating a constructive forest policy to be introduced at the coming session of the Idaho legislature.--University of Idaho Forestry Bulletin.

- - - - - - -

Gipsy Moth Encounters Opposition in New York

Henry L. McIntyre, supervisor of gipsy moth control of the Conservation Commission for New York, who is in active charge of the work of keeping this most dangerous forest, fruit and shade tree pest out of New York State, says:

"More than one hundred men are now actually engaged in the Hudson Valley in the battle to keep the gipsy moth out of New York State. During the summer months quite an extensive survey of the State west of the Hudson River in search of this insect, failed to reveal its presence, which at the present time indicates that the danger of an invasion of the State by this pest is still confined to the Hudson Valley. Present indications are that complete eradication of all colonies found in the barrier zone area in New York State has been secured. Equally encouraging reports have been received from the Federal Bureau of Entomology on conditions in the section of the barrier zone in New England over which they have supervision."--N. Y. Seed Tree.

- - - - - - -

-13-

New Hampshire State Forest Area

The State now owns forty-seven separate tracts of forest land comprising a total acreage of 20,133 acres. Three of these - Crawford Notch, Cardigan Mountain, and A. E. Pillsbury reservations each contain more than 2,000 acres.--N.H. News Letter.

- - - - - - -

A New Game Preserve in Indiana

The Fish and Game Division of the Indiana Department of Conservation has recently made negotiations for the purchase of a 7,600-acre tract in Brown County, one of the hilly sections of the State, for use as a game preserve. A large part of this tract is forested and has excellent cover for game. It is planned to reintroduce some wild turkeys and other game birds and animals once native to this region on this preserve. Hunting will not be allowed.

The Division of Forestry expects to cooperate with the Fish and Game Division to reforest certain portions of the game preserve and bring it into good timber-growing condition. By means of this game preserve the Department of Conservation hopes to keep for all time specimens of the wild life that originally frequented the Indiana hills and at the same time demonstrate the possibility of growing timber-producing trees on land that has been termed "too poor to grow trees."--Geo. R. Phillips, Asst. State Forester, Indiana.

- - - - - - -

Figuring Up Forest Values in Pennsylvania

The question has frequently been asked, "What is the probable value of the forests in Pennsylvania?" With as few definite figures as we now have showing actual forest conditions, both with respect to area and content, the best answer that can be made to this question is nothing more than a reasonable guess. We know that there are approximately 13 million acres of forest lands within the State. This includes large bodies of forests as well as the small woodland tracts scattered throughout the farming districts. Assuming that 3 million acres will not return any wood volume production we have left 10 million acres of productive forest land. Under practical and reasonable management these 10 million acres are capable of yielding 80 cubic feet per acre per annum. Assuming that this annual crop of wood is worth to the owners of the land the low average of 3¢ per cubic foot, we have an annual wood crop stumpage value of 24 million dollars. Capitalizing this possible annual income at 6 per cent, we have a capitalization of woodland production amounting to 400 million dollars and it is this possible wood crop value and capitalization with which we are concerned in the protection of forests from fire. If on the other hand the annual wood crop stumpage value is capitalized at a low and safe rate of interest close to the rate of interest which is actually obtained from farm investments, namely 3 per cent, it shows a capitalization value of 800 million dollars.

Taken from another standpoint, we have the consideration of what the possible outlay in wages would be annually if 10 million acres of forest land in Pennsylvania are satisfactorily protected and reasonably cared for. We may reasonably assume that it will cost on the average of $2.00 to cut the annual production on each acre, $3.00 for transportation, $15.00 for manufacturing, $3.00 for selling manufactured production, making a total outlay on the acre annual production of $23.00 or a total outlay in wages on account of the production of the 10 million acres of 23 million dollars. These figures of course are estimates but I believe they are reasonable. Even allowing for considerably lower rates there is no question as to the fact that the productive forces of nature as expressed in our forest resources are of immense value to their owners and to the commonwealth and that the economic necessity for their protection, considered purely and simply from the value of the annual wood crop, is fully demonstrated.—— Geo. H. Wirt in Penn. Service Letter.

- - - - - - -

Unusual Drought in Louisiana

Thirty parishes in the wooded areas of Louisiana suffered intensely from the drought during the autumn. Although many forest fires were prevalent, the loss did not exceed 10 per cent of the total area protected. Landowners, lumbermen, railroads and other agencies gave the foresters splendid cooperation in holding down the loss.

Clouds of sand blown from the large sand bar on the Louisiana side of the Mississippi River at Natchez so obscured the river for a few days that boats navigating within three miles of Natchez were compelled to sound fog signals to avoid collision. Rivermen say that this is the first time that the river has been so dusty that one could not see across the stream.——La. Conservation News.

- - - - - - -

Bona Fide Natives of Alabama

Wild pecan trees have recently been found in the vicinity of Uniontown, Alabama, measuring approximately four feet in diameter. Men who have lived in the vicinity for over seventy years stated that when they were small children trees equally as large as these were very abundant. The native pecan is among the most valuable of forest trees. Of late years there has been a question raised as to whether the wild pecan was native to Alabama. Early botanists included the tree among those indigenous to the State, but the latest books on the distribution of forest trees omit reference to the pecan in the forests of Alabama.

-15-

To settle this question, Dr. Roland M. Harper of the Alabama Geological Survey and Major Page S. Bunker, State Forester, made a field examination through the sections of the State where the pecan had been reported as existing in a natural wild state. The large specimens discovered and the testimony of the old inhabitants indicate beyond a doubt that the wild pecan existed in Alabama long before any probability of its being introduced into this State from other regions. This most interesting and valuable tree has therefore been officially entered on the list of native Alabama trees.—Ala. State Commission of Forestry.

- - - - - - -

Arbor Day Prize

District Forester Hogeland in a special letter addressed to all the school teachers of his district, called attention to the fall Arbor Day, October 24. He offered three prizes of $1 each for the three largest collections of tree leaves, properly named. Simple rules for the guidance of the contestants were outlined and prizes will be awarded as soon as the identification of leaves can be checked and the winners determined. The names of the pupils winning the contest will be sent to the teachers of each school. This prize idea was a feature of Arbor Day in the Sinnemahoning Forest District.—Penn. Service Letter.

Slight Fire Damage to Montana Timber

R. P. McLaughlin, State Forester of Montana, reports that less than $1,000 damage was sustained to Montana State timber during the fire season of the present year. There were but two fires on the half-million acres of timberland owned by the State.—The Timberman.

- - - - - - -

A Burning Editorial Comment

An editorial in The New York Times says: "Bad as is the destruction by forest fires in the Eastern States this year, due to the excessively dry autumn which made the leaves and grass almost as inflammable as tinder, it is but a repetition of what has happened many times before since the white men first pushed the line of civilization westward. The Indians, more chary with fire than ourselves, never caused the wanton damage that so many white men have done, to their shame; and, although lightning has often started a blaze, the destruction from natural causes never equalled that which results from the carelessness and negligence of our own people. The forest area of the United States is estimated at about 550 million acres. Of this, according to Messrs. Zon and Sparhawk, two of the principal forestry experts in the country, about half has no fire protection of any sort. In

the remainder, which is composed of National and State forests and a few
large preserves belonging to great lumber companies, a handful of rangers
are kept and watch towers have been built. All of this is a recent development. It came too late to save the vast areas in Michigan, Wisconsin and
Minnesota, which have been burned up during the last half century. The
forests in New Jersey and New York have suffered irreparable injury this
season. Due to the dry soil, there has been more underground burning than
usual; with the result that not only are the roots of the trees and plants
destroyed, but the dried vegetable matter in the soil itself has been
scorched. This means that it will be years before such areas can be re-
forested..."--Daily Digest, Department of Agriculture.

- - - - - - -

Setting the Pace as Well as Trees in New York

The New York State Forestry Association has actually planted more
than 25,000 trees on the hundred acres of land purchased by the N. Y. State
Federation of Women's Clubs at South Glen Falls, N. Y., known as the Women's
Federation Forest, the first of its kind in the United States. The planting work will be completed in the spring at which time 75,000 more trees
will be set out. Actual planting is being done mainly by the Boy Scouts.

The Federation Forest is of practical interest because the women of
the State have launched a campaign whose goal will be "A Federation Forest
in every county of the State." They will be led in this work by the Forestry Association, with the hearty cooperation of the State Conservation
Commission.--N. Y. Seed Tree.

- - .. - - - -

To Assist Woodlot Owners

The Alabama Commission of Forestry announces that Mr. Charles F.
Fuechsel, an agent of the Commission, has been assigned to the work of as-
sisting farmers and other owners of small forest areas in connection with
handling and developing their woodland holdings. The aid extended to the
owners of small tracts by the State Commission of Forestry is without cost
to the landowners. Farmers and others who desire assistance in this connection may obtain it by addressing the State Forester at Montgomery.--Agri-
cultural Bulletin issued by Atlanta and West Point Railroad Co., The Western Railway of Alabama, Georgia Railroad.

- - - - - - -

Data on The Forest Fires of 1924 in Idaho

FIRES: Causes

		Classes	
Lightning	921	A	1200
Railroads	146	B	333
Camp fires	191	C	284
Smokers	236		
Brush burning	146	Total	1867
Incendiary	15		
Lumbering	89	Class A - less than ¼ acre.
Miscellaneous	59	Class B - ¼ acre to 10 acres.
Unknown	64	Class C - over 10 acres.

Total .. 1867

	Timber burned M. feet B.M.	Young growth killed acres	Damage to logs, improvements, etc.
National Forest land	12,000	13,500	$8,600
Other lands	17,480	10,350	55,000
Totals	29,480	23,850	$63,600

	Total acreage	Area burned 1924	Percentage burned 1924
National Forest lands	20,616,000	38,273	.0018
All other forest lands	2,324,000	69,688	.0299
Totals	22,940,000	107,961	.0048

The great outstanding needs for better forestry in Idaho are:

(1) Constructive new forestry legislation.
(2) Technical forest administration permanently free from political vicissitudes.
(3) Additional funds for fire protection.

KEEP FIRES OUT OF IDAHO FORESTS - IT CAN BE DONE.

--Idaho Forestry Bulletin.

- - - - - - -

-18-

Battling the Gipsy Moth in New Jersey

When the gipsy moth was first discovered in New Jersey in 1920 it
was found, after preliminary scouting, to occur over an area of about 100
square miles. After the first year's scouting the area was found to be
approximately 400 square miles. In this area, 855 colonies, totaling over
3 million egg masses, were found and destroyed. After the first year's
scouting and spraying work had been done, the territory was again scouted
and 216 colonies, totaling 909 egg masses, were found. The infested
area continued to remain at approximately 400 square miles. After two
years of extermination work, 98 colonies, totaling 1,182 egg masses, were
found which then occupied about 250 square miles. After three years of
extermination work, a scouting of the territory resulted in finding 48 colonies, totaling 723 egg clusters. The infested territory has been reduced
to less than 200 square miles.--Insect Pest Survey Bulletin.

- - - - - - -

Forestry Convalescing at a State Hospital

For the past two years ten acres of the forest land belonging to the
Wernersville State Hospital, Pennsylvania, have been worked over carefully
and all blighted chestnut and other dead trees have been removed. In-
jured trees, as well as defective and inferior trees, have been cut out.
The large logs are taken to the sawmill operated by the institution and
cut into lumber. The smaller material is cut into firewood. No healthy
trees are cut. All the tops and branches that are left after the cutting
operation are piled and burned.

Each spring following the winter's cutting operation all open places
in the forest are restocked by planting white pine, Norway spruce, Scotch
pine, and white ash. More than 90 per cent of the trees planted during the
past three years are growing and in a thrifty condition. Plans have been
made for continuing the improvement work during the coming winter, when 10
additional acres will be worked over and put in shape for planting during
the spring of 1925. All the cutting, logging, and planting work is done
by inmates of the institution. Most of the trees used in the planting are
grown in the small forest tree nursery that is maintained at the institution in cooperation with the State Department of Forests and Waters. The
inmates at the institution also take care of the nursery, which includes
the sowing of the seed, cultivating and weeding the trees, and lifting and
packing them for shipping.--Penn. Service Letter.

- - - - - - -

Current Work on Currants

Since the inception of the Western Blister Rust program, nearly 7700
plantings of cultivated black currants have been eradicated in the West.
The number of plants eradicated is over 118,000. In Idaho alone, over 750
plantings, representing nearly 5,000 bushes, have been removed. The States
of Idaho and Oregon have passed definite legislation, making it unlawful to
possess, propagate or sell cultivated black currants.--Idaho Forestry Bulletin.

- - - - - - -

Foresters Hold Sectional Convention

A meeting known as the Ohio Valley Section of the Society of American Foresters was held recently at Clifty Falls, Indiana. Foresters from Ohio, Kentucky, Illinois, Michigan, Wisconsin, and Indiana were present, and several spoke of the forestry problems of their individual States.—American Lumberman.

- - - - - - -

To Prolong the Lives of Fence Posts in Illinois

Farmers in Illinois require annually 20,530,000 fence posts for renewals, and the Natural History Survey, Urbana, estimates the number of posts in place at 200,163,000 in 625,506 miles of fence, equivalent to 25 times the earth's circumference. About 50 per cent, or 10,931,860 posts, of the total yearly requirements are obtained from native woodlots, the balance being imported creosoted yellow pine and other species of wooden posts. By adopting preservative treatment of fence posts and thus extending their life to an average of 20 or more years instead of 10 or less, the Natural History Survey believes the farmers of Illinois can produce enough fence posts at the present rate to supply their own requirements from native woodlots.

Of late, the supply of post timbers of the more durable species, such as mulberry and white oak, in the woodlots, has been nearing the point of exhaustion. This has increased the use of several less durable species for posts, principally red or black oak, elm, and even much trees as cottonwood, willow, ash, and maple. All these species are short lived in the ground, and it does not pay to set them unless first treated with preservatives. It is also probable that sapling or second growth white oak will not last in the ground much over eight years, hence it will pay to treat such posts as well as those of the less durable species.—Wood Preserving News.

- - - - - - -

A Harvest Challenge

Arthur Herbert Richardson, Forester for the Department of Lands and Forests of Ontario, writes that "In the fall of 1923 we gathered over 3,000 bushels of red pine cones, and it has occurred to me that this might be a record for this species. Do you know of any one organization that gathered more than this in one year?"—Penn. Service Letter.

- - - - - - -

A Reel Record

K. E. Kimball, District Forester

One of the district foresters of the State Forest Service Department of the North Carolina Geological and Economic Survey claims the record for showing a forestry film. "Pines That Come Back" was shown 45 times in three days (19 times in one day) at a recent county fair in eastern North Carolina. Not as many people stopped to view the forestry exhibit as the attendant of the booth desired. The moving picture machine was part of the exhibit so he started it going. The hall was gloomy enough so the electric lights were necessary during the day· The screen was a 30-inch square of white cardboard. The lantern was some twelve feet away. A bright picture about two feet square was shown· It is estimated that over 3000 people saw more or less of the reel and carried away a definite idea of the forestry exhibit. Many more must have received some impression.

- - - - - - -

New Orleans Meeting of the Association of State Foresters

Chapin Jones, Forester for Virginia, Sec.-Treas.

The fifth annual meeting of the association of State Foresters held at New Orleans December 1-4 was very successful and helpful· The following program was given:

Address of Welcome, State Senator Henry E. Hardtner.
President's Address, V. H. Sonderegger, Forester for Louisiana.
Clarke-McNary Law, Col. W. B. Greeley, Forester U. S. Forest Service.
Weeks Cooperation and Fire Prevention (informally presented)
     J. G. Peters, Assistant Forester, U. S. Forest Service.
Recreational Sites in the State Forest, Major R. Y. Stuart, Forester for
     Pennsylvania.
Extension Forestry, G. H. Collingwood, Extension Forester, U. S. Depart-
     ment of Agriculture.
Extension Forestry under State Supervision, W. A. L. Bazeley, Commissioner
     of Conservation and State·Forester, Mass.
Developing Association Efficiency, R. P. McLaughlin, Forester for Montana.
Responsibility of Reforestation, Major P. S. Bunker, Forester for Alabama.
Forest Taxation, G. M. Conzet, Forester for Minnesota.
Forest Taxation, Mrs. Florence Stone, Southern Pine Association.
Secretary's Report, Chapin Jones, Forester for Virginia.

A feature of the formal program was the address of Colonel Greeley on "Cooperation between Federal Government and the States under the Clarke-McNary Law." Col. Greeley had at hand the tentative statement of administrative policy, which he went over thoroughly, explaining many of its new provisions and answering numerous requests for information from the State Foresters.

Another special feature of the meeting was the quite unusual opportunity given to the State Foresters to see the exceedingly interesting and significant experiments in forestry that are being conducted at Bogalusa and Urania. The hospitality of Col. W. H. Sullivan and his associates for the Great Southern Lumber Company and of Senator H. E. Hardtner for the Urania Lumber Company was quite exceptional, and the members of the staff of the Southern Forest Experiment Station of the U. S. Forest Service also were very helpful to the State Foresters in explaining the research work in progress in those places. I think I can speak for the other State Foresters in saying that Bogalusa and Urania fully came up to their advance notices, which is going some.

Splendid publicity was given by the New Orleans press and Lumber Trade journals were also represented.

The resolutions adopted were as follows:

1. Resolved, that in view of the tremendous losses from forest fires which have occurred throughout the United States this year, we, the members of the association of State Foresters, unanimously urge the committees on appropriations of both branches of Congress to allot a sum of not less than $1,000,000 for cooperation with the States in forest fire prevention under the Clarke-McNary law, in the budget about to be considered.

2. Whereas the Clarke-McNary law was intended, supported and passed as a forestry law, and whereas in most States the regularly established State forestry department is vested with the special and sole authority for the execution of the State's forestry law and policy, be it resolved by the association of State Foresters that the cooperation of the Federal Government on all matters pertaining to forestry with the respective States under the Clarke-McNary law should be through the State forestry departments, where such departments exist.

3. Resolved, by the Association of State Foresters at its Fifth Annual Meeting, December 4, 1924, that it is the sense of this meeting that a copy of the resolution passed by the association concerning the Clarke-McNary law be sent to Col. W. B. Greeley, Forester, U. S. Forest Service, with the request that a committee of the association be given the opportunity to confer with him and through him with the U. S. Secretary of Agriculture in support of the resolution adopted and transmitted.

4. Whereas the Association of State Foresters at its Fifth Annual Meeting has received marked assistance in its deliberation through the information and suggestions received from Col. W. B. Greeley and his associates in the U. S. Forest Service, be it resolved that the association hereby expresses its appreciation and thanks to them for their attention and cooperation.

5. Whereas the success of this meeting has been very largely due to the foresight, thoughtfulness and energy of State Forester V. H. Sonderegger of Louisiana; be it resolved that we hereby express our thanks for his splendid and efficient management of all the arrangements affecting the meeting.

6. Whereas the hospitality of the people of Louisiana has greatly added to the effectiveness and enjoyment of this meeting; be it hereby resolved that we tender this expression of thanks to those who have so generously extended true southern welcome and hospitality to us, particularly the Division of Forestry of the Louisiana Department of Conservation, the Lumbermen's Club of New Orleans, the Southern Pine Association, Col. W. H. Sullivan and his associates in the Great Southern Lumber Company and Senator Henry E. Hardtner and his associates in the Urania Lumber Company.

Officers elected for the ensuing year were as follows:

President, M. B. Pratt, Sacramento, California.
Vice-President, C. P. Wilbur, Trenton, N. J.
Sec.-Treas., Chapin Jones, University, Va.

Additional members of the Executive Committee:

V. H. Sonderegger, New Orleans, La.
Edmund Secrest, Wooster, Ohio.

- - - - - - -

Forest Trees for Distribution

The following forest trees will be given away during the spring of 1925 by the Pennsylvania Department of Forests and Waters for planting on idle lands in Pennsylvania:

Softwoods			Hardwoods		
Kind	Age	Height (inches)	Kind	Age	Height (inches)
Pitch pine	2	7-12	White ash	1	8-18
Scotch pine	2	7-10	Black locust	1	8-24
Larch	2	6-12			

These trees may seem small to the inexperienced planter, but twenty years practice in forest tree planting has shown conclusively that the best and most economic results are attained by planting small but stocky and thrifty trees. Shipment will be made by age and not by height.

These trees have been grown for wood production. They are not suited in size and shape, and cannot be furnished for planting around private residences, on cemetery lots, in private parks or on other private lands for shade and ornamental purposes.--Penn. Service Letter.

Island Chronicles

In his annual report, Arthur F. Fischer, Director of Forestry, Philippine Islands, recommends giving greater impetus to the policy of permanent forest reserves; changing the legislation affecting communal forests in order to give them the status of forest reserves; delegating authority for the enforcement of forest legislation to the Director of Forestry; establishing at least six forest experiment stations throughout the Islands; providing a forest products laboratory for the Division of Investigation; making funds available for adequate reforestation of watersheds; placing a larger teaching staff and sufficient equipment at the Forest School; and increasing the personnel of the Bureau, particularly in the ranger group.

The Bureau of Forestry has a field and office force of 5 foresters, 4 forest supervisors, 72 rangers, 46 forest guards, and 13 clerks.

The reforestation problem of the Philippine Islands divides itself into four main heads:

(1) Reforestation of all absolute forest lands not included within the communal forests.

(2) Reforestation of communal forests.

(3) Reforestation of forest lands privately owned whose owners desire to devote themselves to the growing of timber.

(4) Cooperation in establishing forest nurseries and plantations.

At the Forest School the present wood collection contains 1,756 specimens representing 112 families and 924 species. Of the above total 481 specimens representing 45 families and 359 species are foreign woods mostly from Borneo, Sumatra, Burma, Sarawak, and the Malay Peninsula, with a few from Argentina, Guam, Cochin China, Java, Australia, and the United States.--P. I. Annual Report for 1923.

- - - - - - -

EDUCATION AND EXTENSION

Forest Needs of Georgia

As in every other project, the first need is for instruction that reaches the individual. In Georgia we must educate the citizens to realize the meaning and value of forestry to him personally. If we could teach the forestry slogan "Use but not abuse" to every man, woman, and child in Georgia the problem would be simple, but this is a hard task and will take time. If we delay longer in putting the "better forestry" program before the people to make them see their destructive methods of logging and lack of conservation, all the virgin timber will be gone and we will have to grow another crop. It is estimated by good authority that there is the equivalent of enough lumber carelessly destroyed each year in the United States to build five-room bungalows fifty feet apart on both sides of a street reaching from New York to Chicago. Our annual loss by fire is 10 million dollars. The Government report says that more than fifty per cent of this loss was in the South. Another authority tells us that the loss by insects is equal to that of fire. Twenty-eight States have organized fire and insect protection. Georgia has no such organization.

Thirty-five States now have some form of forest legislation. Although Georgia is one of the best timber-growing States in the Union, she will never make much headway until we have a State Department of Forestry with a State Forester and an adequate number of helpers situated in different sections of the State. We should have our State nursery where seedlings could be grown and distributed at cost.

The State of Georgia should have a State forest located in the mountains where forest products could be grown, where the people could find cool camping grounds, and where the headwaters of our streams would be protected, insuring us a constant flow and non-erosion of the land. The control of woods fires is absolutely necessary before we can practice forestry in Georgia. In order to stop these we must have two things; a strong public sentiment for better forestry protection, and the enactment of adequate timber protective laws.

In addition to fire prevention, the forest lands need only one thing to grow another crop of timber and that is time. Time runs into money with our present tax laws. Why should we tax our timber crop 20-30-40 times when cotton, corn and such crops are taxed only once? This can be cared for by a Forest Contract Act.

There are 27 States receiving Federal aid in cooperation forestry work.

The last session of the U. S. Congress made an increase of $2,700,000 available to States having certain forest laws. Why can't our State get forest legislation and her portion of this "Federal Aid" money? Until Georgia creates a public sentiment which will secure forest legislation we cannot get our share of this Federal aid.

There are a number of organizations doing all they can for the forests of Georgia and I think a few of them should have mention here. The Georgia Forestry Association has accomplished more than any other organization along this line; the Federation of Women's Clubs has done splendid work; the Parent-Teacher Associations are very active; and the Georgia State College of Agriculture not only produces expert foresters at its school of forestry but employs an Extension Forester.

Let me briefly summarize some of the "Forest Needs of Georgia";

Education in forest conditions and their betterment.

A Department of Forestry, with a State Forester and his helpers.

State nursery and extension foresters to promote forestry and advise the farmer.

Adequate laws of protection and taxation.--DePre Barrett, Extension Forester, Georgia State College of Agriculture, in the Agricultural Bulletin, Atlanta and West Point R. R. Co., Western Railway of Alabama, Georgia Railroad

- - - - - - -

Forest Taxation Study in Michigan

Professor A. K. Chittenden of the Michigan Agricultural College with Karl Dressel, Graduate Assistant, is making a study of forest taxation in Michigan. They have covered so far the results obtained from the woodlot tax act of 1917. It was found that only 91 tracts are listed under this act. Eighty-five per cent of the woodlot owners so far interviewed expressed themselves as being satisfied with the operation of the act. Mr. Dressel is carrying on a field study in several typical townships in the northern part of the State with a view to determining what the present forest tax situation actually is.

- - - - - - -

Increase in Number of Forestry Students at Cornell

The registration of professional forestry students this year is exceptionally gratifying, 124 signing up with the Department of Forestry, Cornell University, Ithaca, N. Y., for the first term of 1924-25. Last year the first term registration was 98. Seldom if ever has the number been over 100 prior to this.--C. H. Guise.

- - - - - - -

The Spirit of Research

In an interesting article on "Research work and its applications" in a recent number of "Nature," the author, Sir William Bragg, sums up the important reasons for research as follows:

"There are various reasons for the encouragement of research: the benefit of the student, the addition to human knowledge, power and riches, and the needs of defence, military and industrial. But I think we still have failed to include the most important reason of all, the real reason of which the others are only derivatives. It is that the spirit of research is like the movement of running water, and the absence of it like the stagnation of a pool. Scientific research, in its widest sense, implies, of course, far more than exploring the question of physics and chemistry and biology. It is not a religion; but it is the act of one. It is the outcome of a belief that in all things which we try to do we may by careful seeking and by a better understanding do them better; that the world, far beyond what we can see of it on the surface, is full of things which it would be well for us to know. It is our duty and our gain to explore; we have always grown by doing so, and we believe that the health of our souls depends on doing so. Shall we sit still when there are difficult questions to solve and when the answers may give us new insight and new power? There is a hesitation which would beg us not to push forward lest we come to think less of the world. As against this, research is an act of faith in the immensity of things. There is no end to the search; it is a poor thought that there might be.

"The spirit of research would drive us all to work to the utmost of our power, believing that the more we do and the better we do it, the better for the work and lives of others. It is vigorous, hopeful, trustful and friendly; it adds always new interest and new life."

Gems from the Recent Ranger Examination

"The creation of the National Forests was due to the formation of the earth, the volcanic outbursts, the climate and the heavy rainfall."

"The Forests started from a stone in a stream. The stone burst in two and soon had twigs which grew into bushes, and then many bushes which grew into trees, etc., which had seeds, and that is the reason we have pins, seders, fur in N. York, West Virginia and California."

"I desire to enter the Forest Service because I like the forest. I like the work of a Forest ranger. I like the out dore life. I am not afrade of work. It is good wages. I want to help perfect our grat forests. Help to save our country, and to keep thousans of men in work."--Cal. News Notes for Forest Schools.

- - - - - - -

Talk on South American Woods

Dr. B. E. Dahlgren, of the botany department of the Field Museum of Natural History, Chicago, has spent considerable time in British Guiana on the north coast of South America studying the tropical flora, and is internationally regarded as an authority on exotic woods. In an address before the Hoo-Hoo Club of Chicago recently, he gave a vivid picture of the vast South American forests of the magnificence of the trees in their natural habitat, and of the rare beauty, durability and commercial value of their woods. Very little is as yet known regarding the South American woods. About 5 per cent of the forests of British Guiana are held by private owners, and practically all cutting is being done on the remaining Government land. The annual exports of all commodities for that country are valued at 60 million dollars, of which only $230,000 are of timber, $193,000 of this latter sum being credited against one species, greenheart.

The outstanding features of the South American forests are the great height of the trees and the thick underbrush. The forests are in most cases of a badly mixed character. The great number of different trees that can grow on small areas is astonishing, and as many as thirty different species have been found on one acre. Greenheart, which is described as a very straight and very tall tree, with first branches 60 to 70 feet above the ground, is at present the most valuable and commonly exploited wood and often represents 40 to 60 per cent of a stand. It is a heavy and hard wood, impervious to water, insect depredations, etc., and is an excellent material for wharf construction, piling and like uses. The average greenheart log, as seen at Georgetown ready for exportation, is 20 to 24 inches square and 60 to 70 feet or more in length.

The second most important commercial wood is carapa, also known as crabwood or British Guiana mahogany, and the third, walapa. These woods also are to be found in 40 to 50 per cent pure stands. Another valuable and abundant wood is purpleheart, so named because its heart is of a purple color. This should make excellent veneer, flooring and stair material because it cannot wear out, is by nature very shiny and takes a beautiful finish. One wood to which Dr. Dahlgren called particular attention is snakewood, the prettiest of the Guiana varieties, which should have a large demand from furniture and novelty makers. These are all very hardwoods, but there are also many other varieties in South America that are as light and soft as pine.—American Lumberman.

- - - - - - -

Traveling Exhibit on Erie Railroad

H. R. Kylie, In Charge of Motion Pictures and Exhibits, Forest Service

A train of private cars carrying exhibit material and motion pictures on forestry has just finished a successful trip on the Erie Railroad through parts of New York and Pennsylvania, and has the distinction of being the first enterprise of this kind as far as the writer is aware.

The two cars of exhibit material were arranged in somewhat the following order:

Types of lands to be forested.
Species to be planted.
Examples of growth.
Care of the woodlot.
Marketing the product.

Seedlings were shown at different ages and methods of planting were demonstrated. Orders for plants were taken by the Department of Forests and Waters of Pennsylvania, and the Conservation Commission of New York State. Motion pictures from both States were shown and short lectures given at each of the stops made by the "Forestry Special."

It was estimated that the average attendance was approximately 400 at each stop, and there were 50 stops. This made an attendance of 20,000 people – farmers, city dwellers, owners of woodlots, high school and grade school pupils and their teachers; in fact, a truly representative group from the communities visited. As a result, some 500,000 trees will probably be planted next spring.

In addition to the exhibit and motion picture work a great deal of peppy advance publicity was gotten out, and the extension departments of the two States have planned to follow up the work done here with demonstration plantings in the spring. What the harvest will be may only be conjectured, but most of us who were interested feel that a great deal of good must necessarily come of it. It was a new undertaking and there is **every** possibility that other railroads may be glad to cooperate along similar lines in the future.

Starting to Plot at Georgia Forest School

The Forest School of the Georgia State College of Agriculture has started an experimental plot in silviculture. Mr. H. B. Mitchell of Clarke County has turned over to this department one acre which was thickly covered with pine saplings. Half of this timber was thinned and the other half untouched. It is the purpose of the department to let the boys who are specializing in forestry study the contrast in growth and reproduction from these two plots.—Agricultural Bulletin issued by Atlanta and West Point Railroad Company, Western Railway of Alabama, Georgia Railroad.

— — — — — — —

Work of International Institute Discussed

Dr. Asher Hobson, delegate of the United States to the permanent committee of the International Institute of Agriculture, Rome, Italy, spoke recently at a special conference of Department of Agriculture extension workers in the Office of Cooperative Extension Work, Washington, D. C.

The institute, which was established through the efforts of an American citizen, David Lubin, held its first conference in 1905. Forty countries signed the treaty prepared by that conference. Now practically all countries of the world are signers of the treaty, which has the distinction of being perhaps the only one involving a considerable number of countries that continued to function during the World War.

In addition to its service in disseminating general agricultural statistics obtained from the cooperating countries, the International Institute is able to collect from these countries requested information which the permanent committee finds of sufficient general interest to warrant the undertaking. Individuals are also assisted in making special agricultural studies in any of the cooperating countries, through putting them in touch with the persons or offices best equipped to assist these particular investigations and through furnishing linguistic secretarial and interpreter assistance when desired.—Official Record.

Pulp and Paper Courses in Demand

Almost 125 men have been enrolled in the pulp and paper correspondence courses given by the Forest Products Laboratory in cooperation with the University of Wisconsin. Most of the students live in the Lake States region and the New England States, but there are also some from adjoining regions, as well as from the extreme South and West.

The courses are primarily for those who have had pulp and paper mill experience and who want the technical knowledge, although such experience is not essential to an understanding of the work. Among those enrolled are

-30-

mill managers, superintendents, chemists, plant engineers, liquor makers, oilers, clerks, salesmen – in fact, practically every position in a pulp and paper plant has been represented.

The courses include the preparation and treatment of wood pulp, manufacture of mechanical, sulphite, soda, and sulphate pulp, and the manufacture of paper. The cost of the courses is from $20 to $25. Additional courses will be announced shortly.

- - - - - - -

Wild Life Director Makes Trip to "Wild West"

Dr. Charles C. Adams, Director of the Roosevelt Wild Life Forest Experiment Station, of the New York State College of Forestry at Syracuse, spent July, August, and September visiting the National Forests and National Parks of the Southwest. He visited the District Forest offices at Albuquerque, San Francisco, Ogden, and Denver, as well as the Southwestern Forest Experiment Station, the Great Basin Range Experiment Station, and the Fremont Forest Experiment Station. Special attention was given to seeing as much of field conditions as time permitted, with particular reference to wild life, research, grazing, recreation, and general Forest and National Park policies.

The National Forests visited were Carson, Coconino, Tusayan, Kaibab, Sequoia, Stanislaus, Sierra, Wasatch, Manti, the Fremont, and the National Parks were the Grand Canyon, Sequoia, and the Yosemite. With regard to the forests he was particularly impressed with the serious and widespread overgrazing, with few exceptions the relative paucity of game, and with the keen appreciation on the part of local forest officials of the importance of game and forest recreation in its relation to securing public support for general forestry purposes. He was pleased to note the widespread recognition of the severe menace of overgrazing. The urgency of greater financial support for silvicultural research was very evident, and the need of extending research to other fields of forestry than silviculture and grazing was equally evident. Several serious administrative difficulties have arisen because of this lack of adequate research and publication regarding wild life and other problems. The enthusiasm and devotion of the men to their work was everywhere in evidence.

- - - - - - -

New Building for Forest Products Laboratory in Canada

Arrangements are being concluded between the Dominion Government and the University of British Columbia, whereby the latter will erect a new building specially for the Dominion Forest Products Laboratory, at the new university site, Point Grey, to which the university is moving this year. A cooperative agreement has existed under which the staffs of the laboratory and of the forestry faculty of the university have mutually arranged for facilities in the laboratory for student demonstrations. The Dominion Government maintains the laboratory staff, providing equipment and machinery. It has recently expanded its field of research to more nearly meet the special requirements of British Columbia woods, and of the lumber manufacturing industry. Still further broadening of the scope of the institution is to be provided for in the new building.--American Lumberman.

-31-

School Children to Buy Forest

A mass meeting of Milwaukee high school students was held recently in the auditorium of the public museum at Milwaukee, Wisconsin, at which tentative plans were made for the purchase of 4,000 acres of virgin timberland on the shores of Lake of the Pines in Sawyer County, Wisconsin, for preservation as a permanent park and forest reserve.

An executive committee was chosen and tentative plans made for the raising of $300,000 necessary to purchase the property. The plan is to reach all the teachers of Wisconsin through the State Teachers' Convention and to enlist their support in carrying the appeal to the 500,000 school children of the State.

Milwaukee educators are of the opinion that no such spontaneous move of such large proportions has ever heretofore originated among the high school children of the nation and have expressed surprise at the thoroughness with which the project is being planned.--American Lumberman.

- - - - - - -

Old Forest Plantations at Michigan Agricultural College

While professional courses in forestry were not given at the Michigan Agricultural College until 1903, an active interest was taken in forestry matters much earlier as is evidenced by the forest plantations established by Dr. Beal in 1896 and 1875. Permanent sample plots are maintained by the Forestry Department in these plantations and yield table data are being gradually collected.

- - - - - - -

A Menace to Minnesota Oaks

According to Dr. S. A. Graham, forest entomologist with the University of Minnesota, the two-lined oak borer is killing oak trees in Minnesota, particularly in the Lake regions. The oak trees of the southern half of the State also are menaced, according to complaints reaching the division of entomology at the university farm in St. Paul. If the oaks continue to die at the present rate, there will be practically no oak trees left in fifteen years, is the opinion of Dr. Graham.--American Lumberman.

- - - - - - -

Registration in Forestry at Penn. State College

The enrollment at Penn. State College this year for courses in forestry is as follows: Seniors, 10; juniors, 10; sophomores, 12; and freshmen, 25. This is not including those taking courses in wood utilization and lumbering, and those in city forestry.--Penn. State Forestry News Letter.

- - - - - - -

. . . .

HENRY C. WALLACE – LEADER AND FRIEND

W. B. Greeley

The Forest Service has lost a great leader and a sympathetic friend in the death of Secretary Henry C. Wallace. Secretary Wallace came to the Department with a deep interest in national conservation, created by his own study of the land problems of the country and by his intimate contact with Governor Pinchot and other leaders in the earlier phases of the movement.

No Secretary of Agriculture has ever had a more complete grasp of the fundamental things which the National Forests seek to accomplish or of the need for a more complete national forestry policy. Nor has any Secretary had a more sympathetic fellow feeling for his associates in the Government work and for their personal needs and interests. He never lost the hearty, comradely feeling of the man who is bred from the soil and thoroughly understands and shares the viewpoint and aspirations of the plain people. It was always a pleasure for me to take up with him the personal problems and interests of the people in the Forest Service because of his quick and sympathetic understanding of the affairs of everyday life. And there was no more delightful experience than to accompany Secretary Wallace in the field, where he was just as much at home in eating a meal at a ranger station, in talking with a forest guard, or in meeting settlers and stockmen, as he was in mingling with the dignitaries and potentates of the land.

Secretary Wallace always had a keen zest for the simple pleasures and everyday interests common to us all, whether it was a fishing expedition, a trip over a National Forest, or a horseshoe pitching contest. And he carried this same broad sympathy and understanding through all of his official duties. Those of us who had the privilege of close association with him will always think of him first as a personal friend.

Our leader and friend is gone, but his inspiration and his work remain. The best possible commemoration of Secretary Wallace will be for us who carry on to live up to the faith which he had in what we are trying to do and to his trust in our ability and loyalty to accomplish it.

. . . .

Board of Review to Study Forest Fires Starts Work

The Board of Review which was appointed to investigate the 1924 National Forest fire record, in order to determine how the Forest Service can profit by the lessons and experiences of the past season, started work on the Shasta National Forest, California, on October 21. Later, the board will visit the Plumas, Tahoe, Sierra, and Angeles National Forests. Members of the Board of Review are District Forester Paul G. Redington, Inspector Evan W. Kelley of the Washington office, Assistant District Forester R. L. Deering, District Inspector E. I. Kotok, S. B. Show, Silviculturist, and Logging Engineer J. H. Price. It has visited the Shasta and Plumas Forests and gone over in great detail the accomplishments of the season and the failures, and made a thorough-going analysis of the fire problem. Although the work is not yet complete, several major conclusions are already evident. The first of these is that we have no real measure of the maximum rate of spread of fires in different forest types on which our field men can make an estimate of the type and extent of control measures necessary. Several fires were analyzed, which started about the middle of the day and reached a size of over 2,000 acres before evening, necessitating the construction of between 8 and 10 miles of fire line to control. Unless the men in charge of fire suppression can know several hours in advance how large a particular fire is to become, there is serious danger of underestimating the resources needed and of failing to control the fire the first night.

Another distinct conclusion is that there must be a serious attack upon the problem of reducing physical hazards by such means as snag disposal slash disposal, construction of more fire trails through large areas of restocking brush fields, along rights of way, etc. Under critical conditions such as existed for a continuous stretch of $4\frac{1}{2}$ months this year, the possibility of controlling fires is seriously reduced because of previous inability to concentrate physical prevention measures in the forests.

The third important conclusion is the vital need for thorough and systematic training of men. Perhaps in no task in civilian life is the penalty for unskillful work so severe as in fire suppression. It ought to be no more impossible to teach men to fight fires than to teach them to wage war and it is evident that serious attention must be paid to this exceedingly important problem.

- - - - - - -

Increased Interest in Ranger Job

A class of 29 candidates appeared for the Forest Ranger examination at Hot Springs, Arkansas, on October 25. This is by far the greatest number ever to enter the examination on the Arkansas and is doubtless somewhat indicative of the awakening interest in forestry throughout the State.

- - - - - - -

Condensed from an address given under the auspices of the California
Development Association by Paul G. Redington, District Forester,
California District, U. S. Forest Service.

First as a necessary background to a few of the outstanding forest
conservation needs, I desire to point out the important place which forests as a basic source occupy in our economic life. Any account of forest values must consider timber production, watershed protection, recreation, grazing and wild life.

Important as these functions of the forest are, it is as the source
of wood that the forest exhibits one of its most valuable relations to our
economic structure.

The East has already exhausted its northern pineries, once thought
"inexhaustible" while its last great softwood reservoir, the southern pineries, is already so markedly declining that the President of the Southern
Pine Lumbermen's Association has estimated that within 10 years that industry will cease to supply more than the demands of its own immediately trib-
utary region. That means that the industrial east, from New York City to
Chicago and the Mississippi Valley, consuming more lumber than all the rest
of the country put together, must turn almost entirely to the Pacific Coast
for its softwood timber supplies. It means that Pacific Coast lumber production must double, treble, quadruple in future years.

Can we supply it? Yes, if we and all the rest of the United States
grow more timber, on every acre best suited to that purpose. But only thus.
Otherwise we small repeat here the present plight of Pennsylvania, "Penn's
Woods," where with millions of acres once forested but now neglected, fire
gutted deserts, growing nothing of value, the whole State produces less
lumber than is used in the metropolitan district of Pittsburgh alone; or of
Michigan, which 25 years ago produced more pine lumber than any other equal
area in the world, but now cuts less than little Connecticut, while its people pay a freight bill of approximately 15 million dollars a year to haul
from our Pacific Coast the lumber which they must have and which their own
once-forested lands, nonagricultural, and now idle wastes, should produce
but do not. And after the Pacific Coast is exhausted, if it shall be, we
are as a nation at the end of our virgin timber supplies.

The problem is, what shall be done with the timberland now in private ownership, rapidly being cut over with no definite plan for insuring
a new crop. The Congress of the United States has recognized the problem
and through the enabling legislation of the Clarke-McNary Act offers to
the States an opportunity to take the first steps in a sound forestry program.

Coming now to the steps necessary to insure growing timber on lands
adapted for that purpose, we hold the following to be of immediate importance:

1. Air-tight fire protection on both virgin forest and cut-over land,
because without this, other steps in the program are futile. This can be
most readily accomplished by embracing the offer of the Federal Government
to match on a 50-50 basis the sums expended by the State and private agencies.

2. State legislation which will give the State authority to require, by practical methods, the adequate and timely disposal of the slash and refuse on logged off areas, and money for strict enforcement.

3. That in the process of logging an adequate number of small trees should be carefully reserved for seeding purposes, and the young forest growth be saved to a reasonable degree.

4. That the destructive methods of high lead and high speed logging now in general use, are incompatible with this program and should be supplanted by those which will make possible the saving of seed trees and reproduction.

These may appear on first glance as arbitrary measures but research shows that they are all practical steps and already accepted as such by operators who are thinking somewhat of the future. They are in the main justified as much by operating economy and efficiency as by the desire to maintain a productive forest. Definite studies show that small trees in most cases do not pay for their cutting and it would therefore be good business, as well as good forestry, to leave such for seed reserve purposes.

Slash fires not only destroy the cut-over lands but in the end cost real money to suppress.

There are admitted difficulties in the path of this program, perhaps the most serious of which is the present over-taxation of cut-over lands. This renders it costly to hold lands for timber production, but I am confident that an early solution of this vexing problem is in sight.

- - - - - - -

The Ranger's Prayer

H. R. Elliott, Malheur National Forest

Oh Lord in Heaven, hear our plea! Give us high humidity;
Spare us trouble, work and pain, send us stormy skies and rain!
Teach the folks these summer days "Prevent Forest Fires - It Pays";
Keep the lightning from our pines, keep the sheepman in his lines;
Make the cowman know his fault when he fails to put out salt!
Teach the timberman to blush when he fails to pile his brush;
Make us wise to understand these new Manuals at hand;
Make our Supervisor wise, hide our boneheads from his eyes;
Hear this our meek request and then we'll do our very best;
Amen!

- - - - - - - -

Using Wood Wastes for Pulp

"Why aren't the poor species and the wood wastes used for pulp?" is a question frequently asked. Apparently the chief reason is because of the high cost of bringing the materials to the mill or in shipping the products to the markets.

The pulp-wood species in the Pacific Coast States, with usually limited lumber values, would seem to offer specially good opportunities for utilization. Markets, however, are largely in the Northeast which in 1922 consumed 81 per cent of the total pulp wood used in the United States, while the Pacific Coast used only 7 per cent. Freight costs on pulp wood are constantly increasing in the Northeast as the supply of timber decreases; in 1922 the cost per cord f.o.b. the mill was $17.55 in the Northeast and on the Pacific Coast it was $10.20. If the differential in pulp-wood costs becomes sufficiently great to take care of transportation on the finished product, due allowance being made for any small difference in cost of manufacture, the eastern market will be open to the western manufacturer. Transcontinental freight rates on paper are also a factor in this development.

In the South the problem of use depends largely upon the location of the material; if it is found at plants unduly scattered, none of which produce it in amounts sufficiently large to support a pulp mill unit, the cost of collecting an adequate supply from several sources soon becomes prohibitive. The large quantities of "lightwood" and pine stumps in this region have potential value as sources of naval stores and pulp. Under favorable conditions the manufacture of pulp from the chips should yield a profit and at the same time place the extraction industry on a better basis. Possibly development would be most favorable if the pulp mill could be located at the extraction plant, thus reducing the cost of transporting the extracted chips.--Forest Products Laboratory.

- - - - - - -

Hemlock - The Bitter Truth

In Pennsylvania they plant 'em to grow into a future timber supply, because they are tolerant of heavy shade, make rapid growth in early life, and are very hardy under trying climatic conditions. In District 1 (Montana and northern Idaho) we give 'em away to get rid of 'em, or we girdle 'em to form a future fire trap - I mean hemlock trees. All of these things done to hemlock trees are "forestry." True, the hemlocks in Pennsylvania are a different species than ours, but not one forester in ten could tell the difference in either trees or the wood if they saw them side by side, or had them made into a box or a newspaper. I wonder if all of us are doing the right thing to hemlock trees.--Writes in District 1)

- - - - - - -

Opportunities for Foresters in Grazing Work

W. R. Chapline, Inspector of Grazing, Washington Office, Forest Service

As early as 1907, the Forest Service recognized the importance of having men specially trained for grazing work study the problems confronting the administration of grazing on the National Forests. Since that date three grazing experiment stations have been established; several men have studied special problems; grazing reconnaissance for the development of permanent grazing management plans has covered over 23 million acres of National Forest land; several trained grazing men are in Supervisors' positions; and there are 33 such men assigned to the Districts or Forests for special administrative or reconnaissance work.

Some foresters used to think it was unprofessional to enter the grazing field of forestry, but many now agree that a highly important phase of forestry is to develop such plans for grazing management of forest areas as will insure adequate reforestation and economical production of livestock, while at the same time providing conservative use of the grazing resources. There is much investigation needed before all the principles of grazing management are known or developed. This is a work which must eventually be greatly expanded. There is at present, however, a job already upon us which cannot await results of needed investigations and which will require many more men. This is the big job of determining the application to specific areas of principles already developed and of securing the results in administration.

In an effort to develop an adequate force for handling the work about 8 to 10 special grazing men have been employed each year for a number of years. There have not been that many added new positions, however, since the demand for men with grazing training for higher administrative positions in the Service, for places in other Bureaus or in State work, and in commercial endeavor, has been such that these new men have been required to maintain the technical grazing organization. There are now 48 men within the Service who came in by the technical grazing examinations. Twenty-seven colleges and universities have entered into the training of these men, 80 per cent of whom are forestry trained; 60 per cent served as rangers or administrative guards before taking up special grazing work, and only 6 per cent, though college trained, had not had forestry training or administrative experience. The organization thus enjoys the benefits accruing from practical field experience and from a wide diversity of technical training, and is moreover thoroughly imbued with sound silvicultural sympathies.

Of those grazing men who have left the Service and entered State or college work, one is now director of a State agricultural college experiment station, one is an assistant director, one is the head of a forestry department, three are in charge of departments of range management, and one is an assistant State forester. Others include the Chief of Reindeer Investigations in Alaska, Chief of the Office of Weed Investigations in the

Bureau of Plant Industry, Chief of Stock Raising Homestead Classification in the Geological Survey, and Game Warden in Charge of the Montana Bison Range.

The grazing phase of forestry work needs many good men. We especially desire foresters with sound botanical training and preferably with experience in handling livestock. It is hoped that other technically trained foresters, including those now in the Forest Service and those yet to join, will consider the advisability of entering the grazing field of Forest Service endeavor. A greater appreciation of the grazing work by forest schools is needed, as well as the establishment of curricula that give the essentials for this work, and where this is not done a greater willingness by schools to allow substitution of the necessary courses so that grazing foresters may receive adequate training.

- - - - - - -

Distribution of National Forest Receipts Among the States

Under authority of the acts of Congress governing receipts from National Forest resources the sum of $1,346,353 will be paid to the States containing National Forest land for the use of the school and road funds of the counties in which such land is situated.

The amounts the various States will receive for county road and school funds are calculated on the basis of one-fourth of the total receipts from National Forest resources within each separate State. The funds for roads and trails within the forests are computed on a one-tenth basis.

Twenty-eight States and Alaska shared in the distribution of the two funds. California will receive $434,889, Oregon $247,721, Idaho $184,277, Arizona $175,014, Colorado $125,280, Washington $124,860, Montana $115,901, Wyoming $99,634, Utah $81,466, New Mexico $68,077, Nevada $35,653, and South Dakota $34,208.

Arkansas will receive $23,002, Virginia $13,276, North Carolina $12,990, New Hampshire $12,732, Minnesota $8,726, Florida $8,311, Tennessee $4,859, Nebraska $3,912, Georgia $3,605, Oklahoma $2,655, West Virginia $1,292, Maine $1,010, South Carolina $569, Pennsylvania $350, Alabama $248, and Michigan $41.

Alaska will receive $42,720, a sum almost twice as large as the Territory received last year, thus indicating a corresponding increase in timber sales from Alaska's two National Forests.

- - - - - - -

-39-

Forestry and the United States Chamber of Commerce

The midwinter conference of the Chamber of Commerce of the United States, which held its western meeting in Los Angeles December 2-3, had for one of its major topics the problem of reforestation in the West. Reforestation is taken in its very broadest sense and includes methods of cutting, conservative logging and other silvicultural practices as well as such subjects as taxation, which affect materially the possibility of the practice of silviculture by private operators.

- - - - - - -

Preserved Pulp for Paper

In spite of the increasing newspaper habit among Americans and the diminishing stand of pulp timber, there is an annual waste in pulp wood equal to about 12 million cubic feet of standing timber which could be prevented by an effective preservative treatment of ground wood pulp.

Deterioration of wood pulps is due to the action of bacteria and fungi which break down the fibers, thus resulting in a decreased yield.

Unless the fungi discolor the pulp and thereby give visual evidence of their presence, the mill man pays little attention to them.

Fungi of this type often cause a great loss in fiber. In one case a mill lost 500 tons of ground wood through decay, the amount representing about 2 per cent of the total production of the mill for that year. Although the loss in ground wood due to fungi varies widely, a 10 per cent annual loss seems a conservative estimate. This means that 142,700 cords of wood or the equivalent of over 16 million cubic feet of standing timber go through the pulp mills every year but yield no paper.

Although this loss can be considerably decreased by the application of the ordinary principles of sanitation, the only effective method of completely overcoming decay is to treat the pulp with some chemical which will prevent the growth of fungi. Sodium fluoride and certain cymene (crude spruce turpentine) and naphthalene mixtures are effective in preserving ground wood. Pine oil, also, may be substituted for the cymene.

Preventive treatments of pulp add to the cost naturally, but this is offset by the pulp saved and the reduced cost of handling pulp which must be sorted before it is sent to the beaters. Pulp-wood manufacturers lose about $2,300,000 annually in wood that goes into rotten pulp. The great loss, however, is to the country in standing timber thus wasted.--Forest Products Laboratory.

- - - - - -

Watch the Southern Pine Beetle

During the past season the southern pine beetle has again become aggressive in the States of Texas, Louisiana, and Mississippi. It is the opinion of entomologists that these outbreaks are coincident with drought periods. The area in which this beetle is active coincides with that showing a marked deficiency in precipitation during the past summer and fall. Some concerns report one to five million feet of timber killed since July. The Bureau of Entomology, U. S. Department of Agriculture, Washington, D.C., is anxious to secure all reports of pines dying from this cause.—F. C. Craighead, Entomologist, Bureau of Entomology, U. S. D. A.

- - - - - - -

Local Timber Shortage in Early Days

Our attention is directed at different times by various writers to the forestry situation in the American Colonies 150 to 300 years ago. Mr. Will C. Barnes of the Washington office has given us some abstracts from a quaint old book, "American Husbandry by an American," published in 1775:

"Another article which I shall here mention is that of timber, which already grows so scarce upon the south coast that even firewood in some parts is not cheap.*** They not only cut down timber but in clearing the ground for cultivation they destroy all that comes in their way, as if they had nothing to do but get rid of it at all events as fast as possible instead of cutting only what was desired for use among them or enclosing or reserving portions of their best woods for future use of themselves and the general goods of the country, points which we have hitherto seemed to have very little at heart ***. It is clear *** that if legislation does not interfere at this point the whole country may be deprived of timber *** which ought not to be the case while any attention is given to the public interest."

Mr. Barnes calls the writer of the above "the Gifford Pinchot of 1775 demanding the establishment of National Forests.".

- - - - - - -

Scattering Seed Information

Reports from Forest officers indicate that the crop of forest tree seed this year is very meager throughout the Rocky Mountain District except on a few Forests. The Black Hills National Forest has a bumper crop of yellow pine seed, and several Colorado Forests report good seed crops of Douglas fir and Engelmann spruce. The Norway pine seed crop is very scant, as usual. There has been a big demand for Norway pine seed during the past few years from State and private organizations to raise stock for forest planting, and the lack of seed has retarded forest planting in the Lake States and the East. A recent seed catalogue gives a quotation of $22.50 a pound for Norway seed. In addition to the Forest Service, the State of Minnesota, the University of Minnesota, and several private collectors are gathering cones in the vicinity of the Minnesota National Forest. William T. Cox, former State Forester of Minnesota, and now a consulting forester and seed dealer, is attempting to make a big collection, and is negotiating for the use of the Cass Lake Seed Extractory on a cooperative basis. He also expects to extract some cones at the Cloquet Experiment Station. At the price quoted above, it should be quite profitable to collect Norway pine seed even though the crop is very small.

- - - - - - -

Honorable Mention

Down on the La Sal National Forest, Utah, they average about one fire a year. Forest values are not extraordinarily high and the hazard is not great. Nevertheless they have the right spirit as shown by the following record:

Man-caused fires, 3; arrests, 3; convictions, 3.

- - - - - - -

New Forestry Films

H. R. Kylie, In Charge of Motion Pictures and Exhibits, Washington Office

Before our New Year's resolutions are all broken there will be released for showing three new motion pictures gotten out by the Forest Service in cooperation with the Georgia Forestry Association, Florida Forestry Association, and the Conservation Commission of Alabama. The three pictures comprise the SOUTHERN PINE SERIES.

The first is called DUAL PURPOSE TREES, and covers the turpentine operations from the tree to the shipping of the finished product. Into these are woven statistics to show the effect of forest depletion on the industry and the plea for its preservation through the practice of forestry.

The second picture is titled FROM SEED TO SAWMILL and covers natural reforestation. There are shown good and bad logging operations, good and bad forestry practice, some statistics on growth, possible profits, and the splendid opportunities for the practice of forestry in the South. There are beautiful southern scenes that it is hoped will make the picture attractive and mitigate in a measure the dryness of statistics and other necessary matter contained in the film.

The third picture is titled PINES FOR PROFIT, and covers the important subject of planting. Examples of fast and slow growing stands of timber are shown, methods of making the seed bed, planting the seed and seedlings, flashes of areas which contain planted stands of various ages, types of land that should be planted, with many reasons why the planting should be done - winding up with the remedy.

The three pictures have the same theme - "Growing Trees."

It will be possible for those interested to secure the loan of these films for educational purposes, and it will also be possible to purchase copies at a price of approximately $40 a reel. DUAL PURPOSE TREES and PINES FOR PROFIT are one-reel pictures of 1,000 feet each. FROM SEED TO SAWMILL is a two-reel picture with 2,000 feet of film.

- - - - - - -

Looks Like All Work and No Play for Jack Pine

Field work just completed on the study of the jack pine growth in the Lake States by the Cloquet Forest Experiment Station, in cooperation with the Wisconsin Department of Conservation and the Michigan Department of Conservation, was undertaken on 70 plots in Wisconsin, 82 plots in Michigan, and 148 plots in Minnesota, a total of 300 plots. Form measurements of 1150 jack pine trees for the construction of taper, form and volume tables were obtained.

- - - - - - -

Wood-Working Difficulties Reduced by Proper Seasoning

Inefficient seasoning is responsible for a waste of from 10 to 40 per cent of rough lumber in the average wood-working plant.

The defects in the lumber may be twist, side curl, splits, honey-combing, or cupping, all of which were developed during the seasoning. Instead of remedying the drying practice it has been the custom to accept these defects as inevitable and to remedy them by cross cutting, ripping, and re-joining parts with glue.

Illustrating such wastes is the experience of a plant which manufactures bedroom furniture and used 5,500 feet b. m. of 2-inch gum a day for posts and rails. Rejection of pieces partly worked up, some after assembly, and troubles in the glue and finishing rooms were finally traced to improperly seasoned stock. An examination of the kilns and the substitution of the proper kiln drying methods for the rule-of-thumb operation removed the difficulty. Thereafter only 4,000 feet a day were required, and machine work and labor were reduced, thus saving the company over $300 and the nation 1,500 feet of lumber each day.

Such cases are not uncommon by any means; it would be difficult to state how much cut-up wastage could be saved through improved seasoning methods.--Forest Products Laboratory.

- - - - - - -

-43-

<u>Excerpts from the Report of the Forester for 1924</u>

The year just closed has witnessed further gains in public interest and support, in reforestation as a business undertaking by
landowners, and in the growing perception of the value of forestry
as a part of diversified agriculture.

The outstanding event of the year in national forestry was the
enactment of the Clarke-McNary Law on June 7, 1924, which takes its
place with the Weeks Law of 1911 and the earlier legislation au-
thoring the creation of forest reserves from the public domain as
a milestone of progress.****

Commercial forces are now placing a powerful pressure behind
the practice of forestry by private landowners. The two great obstacles in the path of this economic development are (1) the fire
hazard to which forests are subject and (2) the danger of taxation
that will make timber growing unremunerative. The Clarke-McNary
Law strikes at each of these obstacles.**** Two additional features of the Clarke-McNary Law seek to bring about (1) for st planting on farm lands suitable for growing timber and (2) the practical
instruction of farmers in forestry. Both are directly in line with
the national movement to make timber a staple farm crop and timber
growing a profitable adjunct of agriculture.****

Among the immediate things for which provision should be made
by the Federal Government are (1) the establishment of a definite
program and fiscal policy for the extension of the National Forests
by purchase, and (2) a concerted drive for the elimination of waste
in the manufacture and consumption of timber.****

The receipts from the National Forests for the fiscal year
were as follows:

From the use of timber $3,036,395.75
   "   "   "   " forage 1,915,561.49
   " miscellaneous uses, including the
    use of land, water-power sites,etc.   299,945.87
          Total $5,251,903.11

The total is less by $83,915.02 than that for the previous
year. The receipts for the use of timber exceeded those for the
preceding year by $314,519.55, and for the use of land by
$27,489.79. These gains were more than offset, however, by a de-
crease of $425,924.36 in the receipts from grazing. The reduction
in the revenues from the National Forest stock ranges was due in

-44-

part to delinquencies and delays in the payment of grazing fees, arising from the depression under which the livestock industry is still suffering in many portions of the West.****

The net area of National Forest land at the close of the fiscal year was 157,502,793 acres. The gross area, which includes privately-owned and State lands lying within the boundaries, was 182,817,139 acres. The net area increased during the year 265,986 acres; the gross increased 717,357 acres, of which, however, 23,309 acres represent recomputations of existing areas based upon more exact surveys and projections.****

Calendar year	Number of fires	Total area of National Forest land burned over acres	Total damage of National Forest land burned over	Total cost of fighting fires, exclusive of time of Forest officers
1921	5851	376,208	$212,182	$454,099
1922	6375	373,214	494,965	607,200
1923	5168	263,848	180,544	276,598

The steady and substantial growth in the National Forest timber business that has characterized recent years continued, the quantity of timber cut last year and the receipts from sales materially exceeding the record for any previous year since the National Forests were established.*** The timber cut during the calendar year 1923 exceeded by 20 per cent the amount cut during 1922, and had a 23 per cent greater value. The calendar year 1923 was the first year in which the cut exceeded one billion feet.****

Throughout the west the number of livestock is slowly decreasing; and since 1918 there has been a steady decline in the number grazed on the National Forests.****

Far from its being true that the demand for range on the National Forests is slacking down, it is fully as strong as ever. With the National Forests able at present to carry only 16 per cent of all the cattle and 30 per cent of all the sheep in the 11 western range States, the demand will continue to grow. It is important to conserve and increase the carrying capacity of the forest ranges.****

The number of people visiting the National Forests for recreation is estimated each year by the local Forest officers. Since no

. actual census of visitors can be taken; the figures reported are   .
. approximations only; but they afford a fairly reliable criterion of .
. the volume of recreation use. The total number of visitors reported.
. last year exceeded ten million five hundred thousand.   In less than .
. 10 years the number has more than tripled.   .

. . . .

Compliments of the Season

The Forest Products Laboratory at Madison, Wisconsin, is very proud
of a letter received recently from which the following is quoted: "The
writer might just say that the pleasant memories of a trip to Madison,
Wisconsin, with the National Hardwood Association in '23 was the reason
for writing you recently. I feel that in the one short day spent there I
learned more of the lumber business than in all the twenty years I have
been in it."

- - - - - - -

Report of Additions to National Forests in East and South

The annual report of the National Forest Reservation Commission for
the fiscal year ending June 30, 1924, which has just been transmitted to
Congress by Secretary of War Weeks, president of the Commission, calls
attention to the fact that the aggregate amount of land which has been
purchased for eastern and southern National Forests now amounts to
2,346,354 acres.   These National Forest lands are distributed in 19 units
in 11 different States.

There are being acquired in Alabama 87,097 acres; in Arkansas 59,731
acres; in Georgia 159,979 acres; in Maine 32,256 acres; in New Hampshire
409,018 acres; in North Carolina 354,427 acres; in Pennsylvania 166,937
acres; in South Carolina 20,166 acres; in Tennessee 269,077 acres; in
Virginia 560,928 acres; in West Virginia 226,743 acres.

The average price paid by the Federal authorities for the total acreage stands at $4.98 per acre. During the past fiscal year lands approved
for purchase amounted to 130,290 acres at an average price of $3.26 per
acre, the lowest price ever paid during any year.--

- - - - - - -

Difficulties of Road Building in Alaska
T. W. Norcross, Chief Engineer, Forest Service

Road building in the National Forests of Alaska is an entirely different proposition from building in the States. If the work is handled in the most efficient manner, the engineer has not an enviable job. There is a vast variety of conditions, not only on Forests or sections of Forests but on the individual projects. Taken as a whole, the work on the Chugach Forest there looks easy, but it is mainly by comparison with the average project on the Tongass Forest. But even on the Chugach, difficult and exasperating conditions are met. One looking for easy road work and lack of variety had better go to the interior region near Fairbanks; even there he will sometimes meet trouble.

The probability is that for the same type of road, the cost in Alaska will always be higher than in the States. The finished product will not show the difficulties met during construction or why so large an expenditure was necessary.

There are many obstacles in the way of the road builder. The main one is water: water from the skies, water in the soil, and running water. Others are transportation difficulties, high prices, remoteness of Alaska, the heavy and frequent precipitation, and the long period of short days. To get trained and experienced highway engineers to accept permanent positions at the Government scale of pay is a difficult matter.

- - - - - - -

Development of Gas Tractor Logging

Gas tractors and big wheels were used quite extensively and very successfully this season in northern California for logging on slopes up to 25 per cent. Apparently one of the best types of tractor for the work is the Best 60 H. P. manufactured by the C. L. Best Tractor Company of San Leandro, California. The Robinson Big Wheels manufactured by the Robinson Tractor Company of Oakland, California, are generally used. Where this type of equipment can be employed the cost of yarding is said to be only about one-half of the usual cost where donkeys are employed.

While considerable swamping is necessary in connection with the use of wheels, on the whole the forest is left in much better condition than where donkeys are employed. No injury is done to saplings, poles and trees left, which is a very great advantage from the forestry standpoint.--Cal. News Notes for Forest Schools.

- - - - -> - -

Oak Studies in Maryland

The Appalachian Forest Experiment Station has obtained fifty plots in second-growth oak and taper measurements on 135 felled trees on a tract of 8,000 acres near Principio Furnace, Maryland, belonging to the Whitaker Iron Company. This excellent opportunity to secure records of even-aged, second-growth oak stands was afforded by charcoal wood operations which have been carried on periodically since the furnace was first established in 1722. Stands ranging from 30 to 86 years old were found in extensive tracts. These are even-aged, well stocked, partly of sprout origin, and have not suffered severely from fire except in parts of the forest burned during the past three years.

Through the courtesy of Mr. Besley, State Forester of Maryland, three men were supplied by the Forestry Department of Maryland to continue work on the oak study, and about 1,000 taper measurements on second-growth oak trees were furnished the station.

- - - - - - -

Tamarack in Young Second Growth

The Cloquet Forest Experiment Station is studying the rate of establishment of stands of second growth after cutting. One factor of considerable interest is the fact that in many of the young stands of second growth considerable tamarack was found growing in the upland, while in mature stands tamarack is very seldom present. The indications are that the tamarack is suppressed and passes out as a factor in the stand at about the 25th year.

- - - - - - -

Piling a Factor in Blue Stain Losses

More than ten million dollars annually is the loss caused by blue stain, primarily because of a reduction in grade accompanied by a drop in the selling price.

A good share of this loss occurs in the mill yard during air seasoning and could be prevented by proper piling.

Bulk piling for periods of time longer than 12 hours previous to placing in piles is especially undesirable as this favors the retention of moistur in the boards, making favorable conditions for the growth of sap stain fungi.

Since ample air circulation about each board is one of the principal factors in reducing stain, it follows that any method of piling that allows greater air circulation will favor the production of bright stock. In this connection, however, there is one fact that must not be overlooked. Where checking due to air seasoning becomes a serious defect care must be taken to pile the lumber so that both checking and sap stain are reduced to a minimum.--Forest Products Laboratory.

. . . .

Excerpts from President Coolidge's Address to the
National Conference on Utilization of Forest
Products, Washington, D. C., November 19, 1924

This conference has been called for the purpose of further
attempting to deal with the problem of our national timber supply. One of the chief items in that problem is the present ap-
palling waste. Some of this waste may be unavoidable - to a
large extent it is unnecessary. The time is at hand when our
country is actually confronted with a timber shortage. That can
be remedied in only two ways; by diminishing the present waste
and increasing the present supply.*** The Government is going to
ask you to consider definite plans for reducing timber waste. It
is going to suggest that out of this conference shall emerge a
program of specific action for timber-saving rather than a mere
expression of ideas. Containing as it does leaders from every
branch of forestry industry and from many interests closely allied
with forest industry, this conference has, I know, the ability
and the will to create such a program.****

The era of free, wild timber is reaching its end, as the era
of free, wild food ended so long ago. We can no longer depend on
moving from one primeval forest to another, for already the sound
of the ax has penetrated the last of them. We like to think that
it took three centuries to harvest these immense forests. It is
comfortable to believe that they will last indefinitely still.
But in reality we have cut most of our timber not in the past
three hundred but in the past seventy-five years, to serve the
great expansion of population and industry, and there is no reason to expect a decline in the rate of cutting as long as the forests last.**** We do not know the forest situation down to the
last acre and board foot, but we know it well enough to make us
think and act.***

There is no easy road out of this unprofitable situation.
The end of free timber is in sight. World competition for the
world supply will leave no large dependable source of imports
open to us. The use of substitutes hardly keeps pace with new
uses for wood; there is no likelihood that we can become a wood-
less nation even if we wanted to. When the free timber is gone
we must grow our wood from the soil like any other crop. Strange

. . . .

as it may seem, the American people, bred for many generations to
forest life, drawing no small measure of their wealth from the forest, have not yet acquired the sense of timber as a crop. These
immense stretches of cut-over land, mostly too rough or too sterile for tilling, have not awakened us to their vast potential
worth as growers of wood. Fully one-fourth of our land area ought
to be kept in forest — not poor, dwindling thickets of scrub, but
forests of trees fit for bridges and houses and ships.****

The Clarke-McNary Law, passed by the last session of Congress,
will, I hope, speedily change the outlook for these neglected forests. It authorizes Congress, in cooperation with the States, to
establish systems of protection against fire; and it authorizes,
among other things, cooperation in tree planting and a study to
develop stable and equitable forest taxation. ****

There are hopeful signs. Yet we have started too late and
are moving too slowly to bridge the gap between cut and growth.
We must adjust ourselves to an era of reduced per capita consumption. We must husband our supplies. Granted that we shall
get into effect a big-scale program of timber growing, it would
be poor business to go to the expense of growing timber if we
should persist in losing a large part of the crop by unsatisfactory ways of manufacturing and using it. Between cutting the timber in the woods and finally putting the product to use, nearly
two-thirds of the total volume is lost. A third of this loss,
it is estimated, can under present economic conditions and with
tried and tested methods be saved — a yearly saving nearly as
great as all the timber our forests grow each year. Saving timber, it is obvious, will not only reduce the amount we must grow,
but if started now on an effective scale it will relieve the timber
shortage and make less drastic the social and economic readjustments this shortage will force upon us. A tree saved is a tree
grown. ****

We hold the resources of our country as a trust. They ought
to be used for the benefit of the present generation, but they
ought neither to be wasted nor destroyed. The generations to
come also have a vested interest in them. They ought to be administered for the benefit of the public. No monopoly should be
permitted which would result in profiteering, nor on the other
hand should they be indiscriminately bestowed upon those who will
unwisely permit them to be dissipated. These great natural resources must be administered for the general welfare of all the
people, both for the present and for the future. There must be
both use and restoration. The chief purpose of this conference
is to discover policies which will, in the hands of private individuals and of public officers, tend to the further advancement
of this already well-defined and securely adopted principles.

An Impressive Comparison

"A hundred years ago a forest fire was perhaps excusable, but in 1924 the human-set conflagration is little short of treason," says the British Columbia Lumberman. Hundreds of good fellows who would consider themselves blacklisted forever if they burnt down the Methodist Church on Main Street have yet to experience the first twinge of conscience when their camp fire or cigarette sets ablaze a forest of fir and cedar hundreds and hundreds of years old.—Portland Commerce.

- - - - - - -

Permanent Program of the Conference on the Utilization of Forest Products

The first national conference on utilization of forest products concluded its sessions on November 21, after mapping out a permanent program and entrusting it to the central committee on lumber standards.

The program of activities as adopted calls for completion and general adoption and application of lumber standards, as recommended by the central committee; development of the application of better attention to the problems of piling, storing and drying lumber, in all its forms; wood preservation treatments; extension of use of decay prevention in pulp and pulp wood in storage; consideration of methods for arrest and prevention of decay in logs and lumber; encouragement of surveys with the object of utilizing waste products through diversified operations; development, improvement and unifying of building codes; improved designs of boxes and crates and other economies, and encouragement of improvements and economies by organized industrial units consuming forest products.

Lines of investigation which, in the opinion of the conference committee, require first consideration are: forest drain loss in the woods; sawmill waste and practices and machinery; best uses of so-called "inferior species"; properties of wood; a timber survey, embracing the supply, amount of land available by regions and classes of soil on which forests can now and later be grown, and the rate at which timber is now growing and the potential growing capacity of the land; wood-using industry survey; forest protection from fires, insects and tree blights, and possible use of tropical woods to supplement American high-grade hardwoods, being rapidly depleted.

The necessity of putting idle land to work in growing tree crops by the cooperation of the States with the Federal Government, through the medium of the Clarke-McNary Law, was pointed out.--Science.

The report and recommendations of the Committee on Permanent Organization and Program, together with copies of the speeches made by President Coolidge, and Col. W. B. Greeley, can be obtained from the Forest Products Laboratory, U. S. Forest Service, Madison, Wisconsin, upon application.--Ed.

- - - - - - -

Big Figures on a Small Article

The United States uses more than 1,500 billion matches made out of wood every year. This is about 37 matches a day for every man, woman and child in the country based on a population of 110 million. Recent statistics from Europe have placed the per capita consumption there at 14 matches a day. The world output costs 200 million dollars and reaches a total of 4,675,650 million matches a year.—The Timberman.

— — — — — — —

The Central Committee on Lumber Standards and Its Work
By H. G. Uhl, Secretary, Central Committee on Lumber Standards

In view of the emphasis placed upon the work of the Central Committee on Lumber Standards by the recent National Conference on the Utilization of Forest Products, this article is considered particularly timely and important.—Ed.

The standardization of lumber manufacture is perhaps the most important single accomplishment in American industry. While lumber standardization originated with lumber manufacturers and was made possible through the support of wholesalers, retailers, and consumers of lumber, it is due to the earnest and enthusiastic cooperation of the Department of Agriculture and the Department of Commerce that the consummation of this effort came about so rapidly.

In organizing for standardization and adopting a program, a conference of manufacturers, distributors, and consumers, together with architects, engineers, and technical men in May 1922 adopted a program which divided the work into the following three general divisions:

1. Simplification of standardization of grades, including nomenclature of grades and species.
2. Standardization of sizes.
3. Certification of quality and quantity for protection of the public.

The Central Committee on Lumber Standards provided to put this program into operation was composed of 8 men selected from the manufacturers, wholesalers, retailers, wood-using industry, railways and architects.

As an advisory committee to the Central Committee, a much larger body numbering thirty men was selected, which is known as the Consulting Committee on Lumber Standards. This committee is made up of experts representing practically every phase of production, distribution, grading, inspection and consumption of lumber. On this committee there is represented every branch of engineering that is concerned in wood specifications.

Another consulting committee, known as the Hardwood Consulting Committee, consisting of 30 members, is working on the program of standardization in the hardwood industry.

Upon the consulting committees falls the great burden of study and working out the program. These committees report their conclusions on the different questions to the Central Committee and if this latter committee approves them, it then asks the Secretary of Commerce to issue invitations to all interested associations to send authorized delegates to a general meeting to act upon standardization proposals submitted by the Central Committee. If the general conference adopts the submitted recommendations, they are published and recommended by the Department of Commerce under the title of American Lumber Standards.

In December, 1923, in Washington, with more than 100 representatives present from all branches of the trade, the General Conference accepted the recommendations of the Central Committee on lumber classifications, grade names, standard and extra standard yard lumber, sizes, methods of lumber measurement, standard shipping weights and other provisions relating to inspection, complaints, degrades, etc.

One of the biggest problems that arose was the question of determining the dressed thickness of standard boards and dimensions. After a long discussion, it was unanimously voted to set up a standard 25/32 inch for boards with 26/32 inch as extra standard, and a standard of 1-5/8 inches for dimension and 1-3/4 inches for extra standard dimensions. The recommendations of the Central Committee provided for a minimum standard and the adoption of the "extra standard" was made to meet the views of retailers who favored 26/32 inch as single standard for boards and 1-3/4 inch for dimension.

At a similar conference in April, 1924, recommendations were adopted relating to basic provisions for lumber grading, odd and short lengths, lumber bundling, definitions of defects and blemishes, lumber abbreviations, nomenclature of commercial species of trees, grade marking, rough dry yard lumber sizes, mouldings, simplifications of working, tally cards, shipping provisions, shingles and inspection service.

Among the important projects now under way are the following: (1) promotion of the program of standardization for the hardwood industry. The Hardwood Consulting Committee, in cooperation with the Forest Products Laboratory, is now working on the subject of grading rules, standardizing size of cuttings used by the different industries, and making a study to determine the dry thickness that will dress to present practice. (2) The Central Committee is cooperating with the Department of Commerce in conducting a survey of the construction uses of short lengths and at the same time the Forest Products Laboratory is conducting a survey on industrial uses of short lengths. (3) The Forest Products Laboratory has recently submitted a report on factory lumber grading studies of softwoods, dealing with the subject of sash, doors and general mill work. The recommendations of this report will be considered by the Consulting Committee on Lumber Standards early in 1925.

The above projects and a number of others of equal importance will be considered at another General Conference to be held in Washington in May, 1925.

Official acceptances of American Lumber Standards have been reported to the Department of Commerce by more than 70 associations of manufacturers, wholesalers, retailers, architects, engineers, contractors, wood users and railroads. Hundreds of individual acceptances have also been reported.

Summing up the progress made in standardization after three years of preliminary work in cooperation with the Forest Products Laboratory and two years detailed study of the many complex problems confronting the industry, it can be said that the standardization of sizes, nomenclature, grades and grade practices of softwoods is out of the stage of conversation and into the stage of practice.

Two great objectives have been attained:

First, by the elimination of unnecessary and often wasteful sizes, the number of actual finished yard lumber items has been reduced nearly 60 per cent, and by fixing definitions of basic grades a firm foundation has been established for grade equalization. Such simplification of business practice means economies of great magnitude.

Second, and even more important, through the operations of the recommendations, the home builders of America are assured the production of standard lumber and standard products maintained by the united force of the industry.

Copies of American Lumber Standards, with a brief history of the standardization movement can be secured from the Division of Simplified Practice, Department of Commerce. The publication is entitled "Simplified Practice Recommendation No. 16 — Lumber."

- - - - - - -

Western Conference on Blister Rust Control
S. B. Detwiler, Pathologist, Bureau of Plant Industry, U. S. D. A.

A meeting of the Board of Trustees of the Western White Pine Blister Rust Conference was held in Seattle, Washington, on December 1, 1924. About 50 representatives of State and Federal departments, Timber Protective Associations, lumbermen and nurserymen were present. Mr. C. A. Park of Oregon presided, and C. S. Chapman of Washington was executive secretary. Trustees from Idaho, Washington, Montana, Oregon, and California were present.

Deep interest was manifested in the progress of the blister rust control work in the West. Eradication of cultivated black currants to delay rapid spread of the rust has neared completion in Idaho and Washington. Announcement was made that the United States Department of Agriculture considers the cultivated black currant (Ribes nigrum) a public nuisance and is opposed to its growth anywhere in the United States.

The experimental eradication of wild currants and gooseberries for the purpose of determining the most practicable methods of local control were conducted in the upper Priest River Valley in the Kaniksu National Forest, Idaho. Approximately 8,000 acres of the white pine type were cleared of these bushes, averaging 53 bushes per acre. Control reconnaissance was also conducted over a considerable area of the Kaniksu Forest.

Other experimental and investigational work has made good progress following the schedule of the ten-year program for cooperative blister rust control activities in the West which was adopted by the conference last year. Quarantine enforcements continued as heretofore; 36 illegal shipments were intercepted.

The meeting passed resolutions urging Montana, Washington and California to enact legislation declaring the cultivated black currant a nuisance, similar to the laws now in force in Idaho and Oregon. The Federal Horticultural Board was also requested to take the most drastic action possible to prevent interstate movement of this nurse plant of the blister rust. State and Federal appropriations in accordance with the ten-year program were also recommended.

- - - - - - -

Let Us Spray

J. C. Evenden reports that a later examination of the spraying work against the lodgepole sawfly and needle tyer in the Yellowstone National Park shows the work to have been entirely successful. A high percentage of mortality was obtained against both insects. However, only the roadside trees were sprayed and there are many square miles of infested territory on each side of the road which will necessitate continued spraying for several years. A continuation of this work on a much larger scale is contemplated for next year.—Monthly Letter, Bureau of Entomology.

- - - - - - -

In Mexican Hardwood Forests
(Aqui Se Habla Espanol)

In commenting on a recent trip to Southern Mexico, where he went on a vacation trip to cruise a million acres of privately-owned tropical timbers, Tom Gill of the U. S. Forest Service, Washington, D. C., mentioned the difficulties encountered in their attempt to get any accurate information:

Timber estimating is a precarious kind of prophecy at best. One is never sure of the outcome - so many things may happen to knock the estimate galley west even in familiar country and among species so well known as to seem old friends.

But there were no old friends to greet us on entering the tropical forests of Southern Mexico. A million acres and more to cruise among almost totally unfamiliar tree species. Not a boundary line or section corner. A country where, so far as we could discover, no white man had been, where even our own Indians were reluctant to go because of unfriendly tribes in the interior.

Two species we knew in all that riot of unidentified wood -- mahogany, king of tropical timbers, and cedrilla of the cigar-box fame.

It was easy enough to lay out our sample acres and turn in a dozen Indians to clear the underbrush. It was not difficult to measure each tree with a diameter tape and take the height with an Abney. But getting the names of the trees was a different matter.

Notebook in hand, I would turn to Pedro, our Indian dendrologist, and pointing to a tree ask:

"Que palo es, Pedro?"

The Indian would scrutinize the leaves, perhaps chop a bit of the wood with his machete and finally say something sounding like,

"Conchun"

One wondered whether Pedro had answered or was merely clearing his throat.

"What kind?"

"Conchun, senor."

The name, or what sounds like the name, was written down. Then the class in wood technology began.

"A good wood, Pedro?"

"Si. Muy fuerte. Strong like iron."

"What is it used for?"

"Oars for the canoes and fish spears."

A crude kind of research surely, but you must remember we were dealing so far as we know with wood unknown among the markets of the world.

Later on, reaching the sea coast, I sought enlightenment at the office of the Mexican Forest Service. Twenty-five samples of wood specimens I placed before one of their foresters. He laid aside the specimens of mahogany and cedar, then pointed with a shrug at the others.

"We do not know these," he exclaimed; "back there," and he pointed toward the mountains whence I had come, "are a hundred species, perhaps more, all unknown. You cannot float them down the streams because of their great weight. There remains no other way of getting them out of the forests. The Indians, of course - they know them. Each tribe has its own name. Sometimes there are twelve names for the same tree. Sometimes two or three species will bear the same name. It is what you call - very confusing."

I remembered our own dendrological debauches back in the States, and agreed heartily.

My Mexican forester made, what seemed to me, a gesture of derision.

"So you will see that these," and again he pointed at my little pile of wood samples, "are quite unimportant."

I thought of our own pitiful remnant of broadleaf forests in the States and wasn't so sure.

Already north of the Gulf hardwood interests are casting about for the special-purpose woods of tomorrow and here not so far away lie billions of feet of at least potential timber. And in face of this demand and this proximity it would seem unlikely that these tropical species shall long remain unknown and unnamed.

- - - - - -

Why the Forest Assistant Resigned

A new Forest Assistant, on leaving for his first inspection trip, was told by his Supervisor to keep him posted.

"Wire me anything I should know," he said.

The following day the Supervisor received this wire: "Arrived safely. Have lovely room at Paradise Inn. Weather fine. Good shows in town."

This was the irate Supervisor's reply: "Wire received. So glad. Take long vacation. Love and kisses."

- - - - - -

Leaves Burner as Monument to Waste

A significant "sign of the times" is reported from Bogalusa, Louisiana, where the Great Southern Lumber Company has abandoned, for all time, the use of its huge refuse burner, said to be the largest in the world. The company finds that all its waste materials are needed for the paper and pulp mills and other by-product industries centered at Bogalusa. The waste burner will be allowed to stand, however, as "a monument and memorial to waste."--American Lumberman.

- - - - - -

-57-

Tobacco Firm to Help Check Forest Fires

First fruits of the efforts of the Oregon State Chamber of Commerce to obtain aid of the great tobacco manufacturers in forest fire prevention has come in a letter from the P. Lorillard Company, in which immediate cooperation is promised. A forest fire warning will be enclosed in each pakage of tobacco that leaves its factory. The letter was accompanied by a sample of the notice to be used, which bears a caution to the smoker to be careful of matches and burning cigars, cigarettes, and pipe tobacco. Sixteen other factories are yet to be heard from. Other requests in the past have been heeded only by the makers of LUCKY STRIKE in their ten-cent packages.--A. L. Crookham in The Northern.

IF

"If you can toss a match into a clearing,
And never give a thought to put it out.
Or drop your cigarette butt without fearing
That flames may kindle in the leaves about,
If you can knock the ashes from your brier,
Without a glance to see where they may fall,
And later find the forest all afire,
Where you have passed with no one near to call;
If you drive your auto through the working,
And cast your stogie stub into the slash,
Unmindful of the danger therein lurking,
Or homes or happiness that you may smash;
If you can leave your campfire while 'tis glowing,
No thought of industries that it may blight,
Or of the billion saplings in the growing
Turned into charcoal ere the coming night;
If you can start a fire beneath a brush pile
When the wind is roaring like a distant gun -
You surely should be jailed without a trial
And labeled as a lunatic, my son."--Selected.

Forestry Investigations of Practical Importance

The Research Department of the Western Forestry and Conservation Association during the past year has conducted practical experiments on the cut-over land of several interested lumber companies of the Pacific Coast.

Forestry research is becoming necessary to the logger because of a change in conditions. The Clarke-McNary reforestation bill, which provides for a forest taxation study and for greatly increased Federal aid in fire prevention, involves most lumbermen directly, and will raise questions about logging methods, slash disposal, policy of fire control around camps, and inclusion of cut-over land for patrol assessment of fire-fighting expenditure.

Another development somewhat related is the appropriation secured by Senator McNary for governmental forest experiment and study in the Pacific Northwest, which will deal largely with these questions. This should be most helpful, but is added reason for the interest of the lumbering industry in the subject and for its cooperation in order to have the right questions wisely studied.

Further is the question of State or Federal acquisition of cut-over land. This will be a question of values for future use requiring expert appraisal on both sides and determination of how far it pays to go to enhance these values.

And, finally, there should be attempt at least to have taxation predicated on actual earning value instead of upon mere demand that cannot long be met.

The company that proceeds only individually, no matter how sincerely, is traveling a dangerous highway. Teamwork for a few years, until public reciprocity is clarified and dependable, is an essential that must be added to investigation.

The investigations fall in three distinct divisions: timber problems, operating problems, and cut-over land problems. But the three go hand in hand, for the prospects of cut-over land are affected by logging policy, in turn affected by timber conditions.

First is appraisal of cut-over land and its possibilities. This goes not only into the condition of the land and its treatment, with its possible uses and costs to the owner, but also into the chances of exchange and sale, with the fullest knowledge of public trends and requirements.

Second, the checking of growth and yield estimates, which can be used reliably and can also be astonishingly tricky.

Third, the handling of fire from the straight protective angle, the reforestation angle, and the cost angle. This touches slash disposal and logging camp fire organization, as well as general patrol policy and cut-over land protection.

Fourth, in many cases, the situation relating to well-advanced second growth in the neighborhood which is about ready for cutting. Often this should be purchased in connection with plans for logging, railroad building and fire protection.

Fifth, mature timber and logging studies, including age of timber, and its bearing on management. Especially important problems are loss through disease, and the prospects of use for low grade material, mixed woods, and unusual species. In some regions diseases and their habits are highly important in connection both with the time to cut a tract and with utilization in cutting.

Before any owner of forest land knows what to do with it, there are certainly four things he must learn; how to value it; how to improve its value; how it might be used; how it might be disposed of. The first step is land classification. Is it more useful for agricultural or forest production? In forestry calculations, what are the climatic and other advantages for forest growing? What species will you get and where will they stand in future markets? How good will the restocking be and how soon will it be assuredly established? How fast will it grow? When will there be a usable crop? Of what products? What are the protection problems and costs; probably greater in the future accessibility and transportation, perhaps better or worse than now? Are there any by-product possibilities, like grazing or thinnings? The latter might increase production besides paying carrying costs. What are the tax prospects?

There is a place in this for all concerned. The Government, the States, the forest schools, and the private foresters have each their responsibility and there is plenty for each to do. It is obvious, however, that loggers and landowners have equal interest and that unless they also take part individually and collectively they will suffer, both individually and collectively.

This is the nature of the service that the Research Department of the Western Forestry and Conservation Association is trying to give you.--American Lumberman. (Condensed from address of E. T. Allen, Forester in Charge, Western Forestry and Conservation Association.)

- - - - - - -

Burned and charred stumps will never contribute toward the building of a great commonwealth.--Frank H. Lamb.

- - - - - - -

Louisiana Mill Managers Adopt Recommendations on Fire Prevention

The Louisiana Mill Managers' Association adopted unanimously the following recommendations submitted by the fire prevention committee of that organization:

(1) The full cooperation of the Louisiana Mill Managers' Association be extended to the State forestry division, Department of Conservation, in their efforts to prevent forest and cut-over land fires.

(2) That properly worded signs be placed at all crossroads, and prominent places along the public highways, as well as at county fairs, public meetings, etc., asking the cooperation of the general public in the prevention of forest fires, these signs to be supplied by the State forestry division.

(3) To work with the police jury in their efforts for the prevention of forest fires.

(4) To solicit the cooperation of the judges of the various districts and suggest that they charge the grand juries with reference to forest fires.

(5) To take up with the superintendent of education and superintendents of the various school districts with reference to teaching the children the hazards and destruction of forest fires, asking their help in the prevention of same, and also suggest that the forestry division take up the proposition with the superintendents of the various schools, asking that the children prepare essays on the subject of forest fires, the damage caused, and methods of prevention, offering, if necessary, prizes for the best papers.

(6) Solicit the cooperation of the press in the printing of articles on the destruction and prevention of forest fires.

(7) Request all civic bodies to help in the prevention of forest fires.

(8) That papers be prepared covering the destruction of young trees, damage to growing timber and land by forest fires, same to be read before schools, civic bodies, etc.

(9) Solicit the cooperation of all traveling salesmen, who travel by auto, in the prevention of forest fires, asking that they report any fires they may see to the proper authorities.

(10) Secure the cooperation of all ministers, especially those in the rural districts.--Southern Lumberman.

- - - - - - -

Footprints on the Snows of Time

An old Chinaman working around a lumber camp heard a noise and espied a huge brown bear sniffing his tracks in the newly-fallen snow.

"Huh!" he gasped. "You likee my tlacks? I makee some more."--American Forests and Forest Life.

- - - - - - -

As Others Utilize the Squeal of Livestock, So Lumbermen Plan to Use the Squeak of Lumber!

The Great Southern Lumber Company, whose mill at Bogalusa, La., cuts 750,000 feet of lumber a day, is now utilizing the product of the tree so closely that wood for fuel is no longer available to the people of the town. This is made possible by the manufacture of paper and other by-products, although waste in lumber manufacture at the mill proper has been reduced to a minimum. Not much more than limbs goes to the paper mill.

Men whose opinion is authoritative have said that the time may come when the products of the tree now inaccurately termed "waste" may prove to be more valuable than the present primary product — lumber.

There is much that is inspiring about an industry that is making the progress that is being registered from day to day in lumbering. It may well be that lumbermen themselves do not realize the number and significance of the advancements being made in forestry, in closer utilization at sawmill and by-products plants and in wood-consuming factories. It is not too much to say that every manufacturer of lumber and every user of wood is concentrating his efforts upon economic production and utilization.—American Lumberman.

- - - - - - -

Test of the Durability of Treated Ties

From 1904 to 1918 inclusive, the Atchison, Topeka and Santa Fe Railway inserted in special test tracks at 16 stations and on branch lines in four States a total of 136,345 creosoted crossties. Of these test ties 112,560 or 82.56% were pine, 15,529 or 11.38% gum, 7,461 or 5.47% red oak, and 795 or 0.59% beech ties.

An official inspection between January 20 and April 1, 1924 — 19 years after the first ties were laid — showed that 130,938 ties or over 96% were still in track and that of the 5,407 ties removed only 110 or less than 0.1% of the total number of ties originally laid were removed because of decay.

Of the 130,938 creosoted ties still in service 24,356 or 18.60% have been in track for 15 to 19 years, 78,125 or 59.66% for 10 to 15 years, and 28,457 or 21.74% for less than 10 years.—"Wood Preserving News" in the N. J. Forestry News.

- - - - - - -

A New Aneroid

G. Paulin, a Swedish engineer, has placed on the market a new aneroid which, according to the Engineering News Record, is much more efficient than any of the present instruments. It covers ranges in altitude from sea level to 10,000 feet and will register differences in elevations as small as one foot. The instrument contains no gears, rivets or chains and it is claimed to be extremely accurate and dependable. An instrument of this character, if it proves as efficient as the inventor claims, would be of invaluable assistance in preparing topographic maps.

Saving and Renewing the Redwoods

A program for the reforestation of redwood timber in Humboldt County, California, is being actively carried forward under the direction of the Humboldt Redwood Reforestation Association. This association, in connection with the Pacific Lumber Company, maintains a nursery at Scotia, California, embracing an area of five and a half acres devoted to seedbeds, transplant beds and experimental sections. An interesting feature in connection with the growing of the young trees is the method employed of pruning the roots to make them stocky. A four-foot saw blade attached to a rail spreader drawn by two horses is employed. It is proposed to plant about 500 trees to the acre. A planting policy covering the next four years has been worked out and the principal species to be grown are redwood, Douglas fir, Port Orford cedar, and Sitka spruce. The planting season is restricted to the winter season months.

The Board of Supervisors of Humboldt County has appropriated a fund of $25,000 for the purpose of saving the redwoods. This amount was provided for in the tax levy made by the board for the ensuing year as the beginning of a "Save the Redwoods" fund to be utilized as needed in completing the Redwood Park system in Humboldt County. The county has already appropriated in the past the sum of $85,000 toward saving redwood timber in the Humboldt State Redwood Park. This brings the total sum appropriated by them to over $100,000. This action on the part of Humboldt County comes soon after the formal voting by the Board of Supervisors of Del Norte County to set aside an annual fund for the saving of redwoods along the State highway. A sum of $5,000 was appropriated by them for 1924-25.—The Timberman.

- - - - - - -

Henry Ford's Utilization Project

Much has been written lately about the forestry efforts of Henry Ford. No phase of his conservation work appears to be more productive of practical results than the closer utilization project now under way.

A tree was taken that gave two irregular logs and scaled 238 board feet. Under the old system of utilization it is estimated that about 127 board feet of "auto" parts would have been obtained from these logs. By cutting them according to the Ford system 204 board feet were obtained, and in addition 170 board feet were also procured from limbs and tops heretofore regarded as worthless except for distillation or fuel. This makes a total of 374 board feet as against 127 board feet from the same tree by the old method.--Penn Service Letter.

Opposed to Increase in Timber Royalties in British Columbia

Strenuous efforts are being put forth by the Timber Industries Council of British Columbia to forestall the increase in timber royalties that is scheduled to become effective January 1, 1925. In its arguments against the preposed advance, the council points out that British Columbia already pays the highest timber taxes in the world. A recent statement issued by the council sets forth the reasons why further taxes are undesirable:

"In no country in the world is the standing timber taxed to such an extent as in British Columbia, and yet on January 1, 1925, the present uneconomic royalty measure that is now in operation will, unless repealed, automatically increase the present rate by 300 per cent, making an increase of 300 per cent since its enactment in 1914.

"Two facts must be recognized. First: a large portion of our timber is mature and should be harvested as soon as possible. To hold up the logging of it by impossible taxation at this stage is to sanction its deterioration. In the second place, British Columbia, although magnificently wooded, has by no means a monopoly of the world's softwood, or even of the valuable species of the Douglas fir area. In marketing its forest products it is in severe competition with countries that encourage instead of taxing the development of their natural resources."--The Timberman.

- - - - - - -

Wool from Pine Leaves

German scientists are reported to have found a way to manufacture material closely resembling wool by chemically treating the leaves of the Scotch pine. It is said that this new substance can be spun, curled, and woven. One of the uses to which it is being put is a stuffing for mattresses. The aromatic odor makes the mattresses insect proof and agreeable and beneficial to sleepers, especially patients in hospitals.

The fir leaves are gathered every second year while they are still green. They are then boiled, and by the use of chemicals the resinous substances are removed from them. The remaining fibers are separated and cleansed of all foreign matter. The result of this process is artificial wool. An oil by-product, differing somewhat from turpentine, but having many of its properties, is also derived.--Penn. Service Letter.

- - - - - - -

Another Fire?

Some rangers blaze a way; others only blaze away.--Six Twenty-Six.

- - - - - - -

. . . .

CHARLES HOWARD SHINN

April 29, 1852 - December 2, 1924

On Tuesday night, December 2, at his daughter's home in Ukiah, Charles Howard Shinn passed on. The funeral was held there Thursday afternoon at 2:30.

Thus much the bare record. But what it means to the California District of the Forest Service, and to all foresters and the cause of forestry in our country, words only haltingly express. No one has said more in few words for him than did the "Sierra Ranger," on that Forest to which Mr. Shinn gave longest and most peculiarly his labor of love, when the Shinn place at Northfork was offered for sale: "That hits — doesn't it? A great love can be crowded into one small sentence — respect, and love, and a tightening of the throat. Peace Cabin is for sale. But the high-mindedness, the fine courage, the inspiration that have come from Peace Cabin, and that are a part of our hearts and purpose, are not in the market. We own the real Peace Cabin. Peace Cabin is not for sale!"

And now Mr. Shinn has passed. But, as truly, his world can never lose him. Other men may serve the cause of forestry in positions of more far-flung responsibility, but few more significantly, and none ever more truly, to his last ounce of energy and life. And to none, we venture, is it given to contribute to his fellows in larger measure of those most priceless possessions of men or organizations, the invisible and eternal foundations of character, spoken of by the Sierra.

With his nearest and dearest we also grieve. But what a solace is the abiding presence of such a life! "O death, where is thy sting? O grave, where is thy victory?"--Cal. District News Letter.

. . . .

E. J. Fenby has been appointed Supervisor of the Rainier National Forest, Washington, succeeding G. F. Allen, deceased. Fenby has been on the Rainier for the past fifteen years as Forest Assistant, Forest Examiner, Deputy Supervisor, and Superintendent of Road Construction. Before coming to the Northwest he was engaged in forestry work in Canada, in the Southern Appalachians, and in Montana. His technical training was secured at Johns Hopkins, and at Biltmore.

- - - - - - -

Professor J. Nelson Spaeth has recently been added to the forestry faculty of the New York State College of Agriculture. Professor Spaeth was graduated from the College of Agriculture at Cornell and had graduate study at the Harvard Forest School. He has been assistant to the director of the Harvard Forest. It is expected that Professor Spaeth will establish permanent sample plots in typical New York forests.--Cornell Extension Service News.

- - - - - - -

Edwin L. Mowat, who has been field assistant on the Douglas fir yield study at the Pacific Northwest Forest Experiment Station, has taken a position as instructor in forestry at the Forest School of Oregon Agricultural College. His place is being taken by L. R. Barrett, a Michigan Forest School graduate who served as lookout on Mt. Ireland, Whitman National Forest, Oregon, last summer.

- - - - - - -

Robert Marshall, the field assistant who worked out of the Wind River Branch of the Experiment Station most of the summer left on October 1 to take a post graduate course in the Harvard Forest School.

- - - - - - -

Samuel J. Record, Professor of Forest Products in Yale University, delivered an illustrated lecture on "The Wonders of Wood" in the James Simpson Theater of the Field Museum of Natural History in Chicago recently to an audience of 900 people.

- - - - - - -

D. G. Rankin has recently been appointed Blister Rust Control Agent to look after Columbia, Greene and Ulster counties, with headquarters at Hudson, N. Y.--N. Y. Observer.

- - - - - - -

Prof. W. G. Edwards is on leave of absence for a year from Penn. State College and is taking post graduate work in lumbering at the University of California. W. E. MacMillan, Penn. State 1923, is taking his place. MacMillan was at Cornell last year doing graduate work in Forestry.--Penn. State Forestry News Letter.

- - - - - - -

New Forester in Hawaii

Theo. C. Zscholke, who recently returned to the United States from the Philippine Forest Service, has accepted a position as assistant superintendent of forestry for Hawaii and has left to take up his duties in Honolulu. -- P. I. Makiling Echo.

- - - - - - -

Student assistants appointed recently to the Southern Forest Experiment Station are James L. Averell and Philip C. Wakeley.

- - - - - - -

Professor Burr N. Prentice resigned recently as agent in Blister Rust Control in New York to renew his work in the Forestry Department of Purdue University.--Blister Rust News.

- - - - - - -

Professor J. C. DeCamp of the Michigan Agricultural College has been one of the guiding spirits in the Lansing Hoo Hoo Club and is also secretary of the Michigan Forestry Association. He is taking up a study of small sawmill operations in central Michigan with a view to determining the character of the product manufactured and a suitable price to charge for cutting woodlot timber.

- - - - - - -

Professor P. A. Herbert of the Michigan Agricultural College is continuing his work in forest insurance. He has prepared an extended bibliography on the subject and spent some time in northern Michigan studying fire risks. Professor Herbert believes that forest insurance is essential before reforestation is undertaken by private companies on a large scale.

- - - - - - -

The following men were appointed recently as Field Assistants in Blister Rust Control, Washington; A. G. Darwin, Cecil H. Hatton, Percy E. Melis, Carl O. Peterson, Mack W. Hodner, Guy J. Scholl, Philip S. Simcoe, Clarence C. Strong.--Blister Rust News.

- - - - - - -

Dow V. Baxter, who has been in the employ of the Blister Rust Control, U. S. Department of Agriculture intermittently from 1918 to 1923, is joining the staff of the Botanical Department of the University of Wisconsin as Instructor.--Blister Rust News.

- - - - - - -

J. M. Bennett, Forester for Wayne County, Michigan, has a considerable force of foresters working under him. He has charge of the parks and roadside trees in the county and has been doing a great deal to develop interest in forestry there.

- - - - - - -

C. E. Baker has been appointed Federal blister rust agent in Essex County, New York.--N. Y. Observer.

- - - - - - -

L. C. Palmer, Forester for the Kent County Board of Supervisors, is in charge of the forest experiment station near Grand Rapids, Michigan, maintained by the Kent County Board of Supervisors and the Michigan Agricultural College primarily for forest planting.

- - - - - - - -

W. F. Damtoft, forester for the Champion Fibre Company, and C. F. Korstian, Associate Silviculturist at the Appalachian Forest Experiment Station, are working on plans in connection with the proposed expansion of the company's nursery at Canton, North Carolina. Experiments on the control of weeds and of damping off have been started, based upon recommendations of the Bureau of Plant Industry.

- - - - - -

Mr. Elmer R. Ford, who has been associated with the Office of Blister Rust Control for several years as Assistant Pathologist, resigned recently to accept an appointment as Valuation Engineer in the Treasury Department, Income Tax Unit, Timber Section.--Blister Rust News.

- - - - - -

During the past season the members of the staff of the Roosevelt Wild Life Forest Experiment Station of the New York State College of Forestry at Syracuse, has been engaged in field studies as follows: Dr. Charles E. Johnson continued his study of the Adirondack beaver, Dr. A. O. Gross has studied the status of the Ruffed Grouse in the lower Hudson Valley, and Mr. B. A. Scudder has studied the Adirondack deer situation.

- - - - - -

Forester O. W. Pflueger, Chief Division of Investigation and In Charge of the Forest School, Philippine Islands, has reported for duty after nine months' leave of absence. During his vacation he visited Yale University, Cornell, and Syracuse University, the Forest Products Laboratory at Madison, Wisconsin, and the U. S. Forest Service at Washington, D. C., and San Francisco, California. He brought with him a good collection of books and pamphlets on forestry which will be used as references in the Forest School.--P.I. Makiling Echo.

- - - - - -

Wm. Clavé, Ralph O. Gould, and Ronald B. Craig have been appointed as agents in Blister Rust Control in Massachusetts.--Blister Rust News.

- - - - - - -

ARTICLES, BIBLIOGRAPHIES, PUBLICATIONS

Recent Books on Forestry

Timbers of Tropical America, by Samuel J. Record, M. A., M. F., and
Clayton D. Mell, B. A., M. F., Yale University Press.

Caoba - The Mahogany Tree. Translated by Walter D. Wilcox. The Knicker-
bocker Press. G. Putnam's Sons.

Isolation a Factor in the Natural Regeneration of Certain Conifers, by
James W. Toumey and Ernest J. Neethling. Yale University Press.

Miscellaneous Publications

Simplified Practice Recommendation No. 16, issued by the Department
of Commerce, deals with American lumber standards.

- - - - - - -

J. S. Illick, of the Pennsylvania Department of Forests and Waters,
is co-author of a new book "A Popular History of American Invention" which is
just from the press of Charles Scribner Sons. He contributed the chapter on
"The Story of the American Lumber Industry."

- - - - - - -

In Volume 12, New York Botanical Garden Bulletin #45, is a 25-page
discussion of "Hemlock and Its Environment."

- - - - - - -

Manual of Tree and Shrub Insects, compiled by Ephraim Porter Felt, State
Entomologist of New York, gives a practical summary of the insect problem in
its relation to forest and shade trees.

- - - - - - -

Valuable information and statistics pertaining to the timber resources
and lumber trade of Canada are contained in the most recent commerce report
of the Bureau of Foreign and Domestic Commerce, U. S. Department of Commerce.
Data for this report were obtained from "Forests of Canada," a publication of
the Department of the Interior of Canada, issued in 1923.

- - - - - - -

Map of Natural Vegetation. Zon and Shantz.

- - - - - - -

The Seventh Biennial Report of the State Forester, State of Montana, for the Short Period December 1, 1920, to June 30, 1921, and the Fiscal Years 1922 and 1923, has been published and is now ready for distribution by that State.

- - - - - - -

Farmers Bulletin #1184, "Currants and Gooseberries, Their Culture and Relation to White Pine Blister Rust."

- - - - - - -

Articles from the Forest Service in Current Periodicals

Benson, A. C. Greater Yield from Logs. Southern Lumberman, October 18, 1924.

Bonner, F. E. The Forest Road System of California. California Highways, September, 1924.

Bruce, Donald. A New Technique for Growth Studies by Stem Analyses, Journal of Forestry, October, 1924.

Behre, C. F. Computation of Total Contents of Trees, Journal of Forestry, October, 1924.

Cleator, F. W. Recreation Objectives in National Forest Administration. University of Washington Forest Club Quarterly, June, 1924.

Curran, C. E., and Baird, B. K. Bleaching of Wood Pulp, III. The Effect of Temperature on the Bleaching of Sulphite Pulp. Paper Trade Journal, September 11, 1924.

Dain, B. D. Weed Trees and Sawmill Profits. The Timberman, October, 1924.

Frothingham, E. H. Forestry and Forest Investigations in the Southern Appalachians. Asheville (Sunday) Citizen, September 21, 1924.

Greeley, W. B. Fire Season on the National Forests. American Forests and Forest Life, November, 1924.
Man-caused Fires Make Staggering Total. Lumber World Review, October 10, 1924.

Griffin, G. J. Further Note on the Position of the Tori in Bordered Pits in Relation to Penetration of Preservatives. Journal of Forestry, October, 1924.

Griffith, G. E. Fighting Fire with Posters. Timberman, September, 1924.

Guthrie, J. D. Development of New Oregon Pine Section. The Timberman, October, 1924.
Forest people: Albert of Eagle Creek. American Forests and Forest Life, November, 1924.

-70-

Krauch, H. Acceleration of Growth in Western Yellow Pine Stands after Cutting.
    Journal of Forestry, October, 1924.

Larsen, J. A., and W. C. Lowdermilk. Slash Disposal in Pine Forests of
    Idaho. West Coast Lumberman, October 15, 1924.

Leopold, A. Grass, Brush, Timber, and Fire in Southern Arizona. Journal of
    Forestry, October, 1924.

Miller, R. N., and W. H. Swanson. Pressure in Sulphite Cooks. Paper,
    October 16, 1924.

Munger, T. T. Lumber from 43-year-old Forest. The Timberman, September,
    1924.

McCarthy, E. F. The Record the Tree Keeps. Wood Turning, August, 1924.

Pincetl, M. F. The Fire at Plum Bar. American Forests and Forest Life,
    November, 1924.

Preston, Jno. F. Forest Practice and Possibilities in North Idaho. The
    Timberman, May, 1924.

Redington, P. G. Highways Needed to Develop California's Forests. Califor-
    nia Highways, September, 1924.

Rue, J. D., Wells, S. D., and Schafer, E. R. Study of Flax Straw for Paper
    Making. Paper Mill, September 27, 1924. Paper Trade Journal, Sept.
    25, 1924. Paper, Sept. 25, 1924.

Sherman, E. A. Military Reservations Will Produce Timber. Foreign Service,
    October, 1924.

Stockbridge, Miss H. E. Bibliography of Douglas Fir. Mimeographed.
                    "   on Erosion.   "

Wells, S. D. Cooperation in Obtaining and Using Raw Materials.
    Paper Mill and Wood Pulp News, October 18, 1924.

Wahlenburg, W. G. Stimulating Growth of Engelmann Spruce in the Nursery.
    The Timberman, August, 1924.

Wyman, L. How Fast Should a Face be Raised in Chipping Timber? Southern Lum-
    ber Journal, October 15, 1924.

Weidman, R. H. Forest Experiments in Idaho. The Timberman, September, 1924.

Rept. 188 – The Influence of the form of a wooden beam on its stiffness
and strength. III. – Stresses in Wood Members, etc.
. (Reprint from National Advisory Committee for Aeronautics)

Recreation

Unnumb. Pub.   Vacation in the National Forests.   (Reprint.)

D-1   Montana's Largest Big-Game Refuge.

D-3   Apache National Forest – Map Folder.

Californial's Recreation Grounds – Litho Map only.

Forest Regions of the United States – Map only.

CPSIA information can be obtained
at www.ICGtesting.com
Printed in the USA
BVHW050040061118
532207BV00022B/2529/P